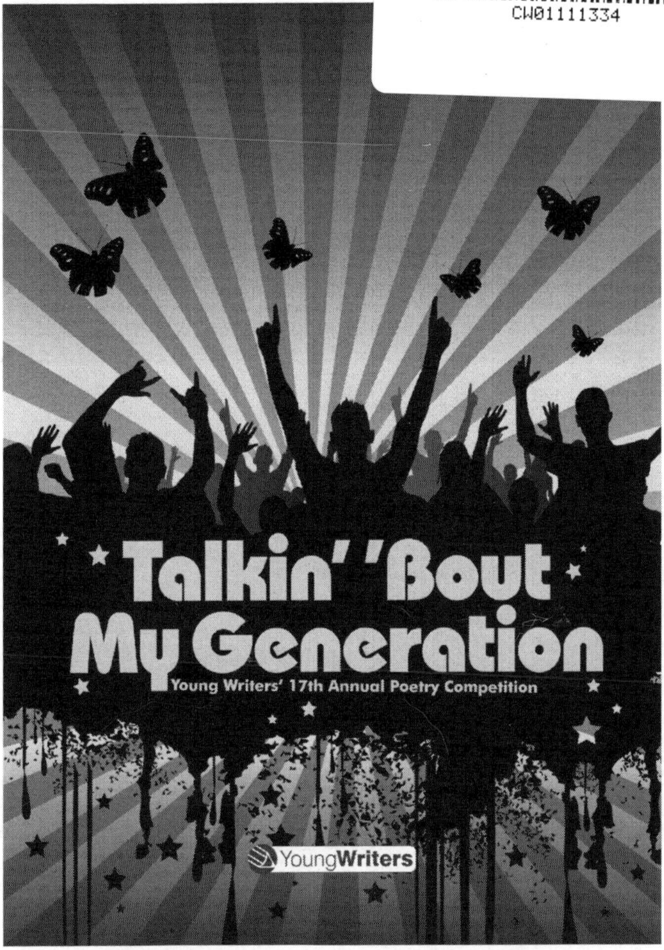
Talkin' 'Bout
My Generation
Young Writers' 17th Annual Poetry Competition
YoungWriters

Verses From Wales

Edited by Samantha Wood

First published in Great Britain in 2008 by:
Young Writers
Remus House
Coltsfoot Drive
Peterborough
PE2 9JX
Telephone: 01733 890066
Website: www.youngwriters.co.uk

All Rights Reserved

© Copyright Contributors 2008

SB ISBN 978-1 84431 702 8

Foreword

This year, the Young Writers' *Talkin' 'Bout My Generation* competition proudly presents a showcase of the best poetic talent selected from thousands of up-and-coming writers nationwide.

Young Writers was established in 1991 to promote the reading and writing of poetry within schools and to the young of today. Our books nurture and inspire confidence in the ability of young writers and provide a snapshot of poems written in schools and at home by budding poets of the future.

The thought, effort, imagination and hard work put into each poem impressed us all and the task of selecting poems was a difficult but nevertheless enjoyable experience.

We hope you are as pleased as we are with the final selection and that you and your family continue to be entertained with *Talkin' 'Bout My Generation Verses From Wales* for many years to come.

Contents

Alun School, Mold
Harry Varney (12)	1
Remi Whelan (13)	2
Kieren Turner Owen (12)	2
James Grundy (13)	3
Nicholas Roberts (12)	3
Gareth Thomas (13)	4
Sophie Greatbatch (12)	5
Beth Lloyd (14)	5
Kristina Waxler (13)	6
Luke Van Der Kooij (12)	7
Cameron Leiper (13)	8
Ben Szulc (13)	8
Molly Reid (13)	9
Stefan Rosier (13)	9
Charlotte Hewitt (14)	10
Anokhi Patel (13)	11
Ffion Rowlands (14)	12
Julia Bond (14)	13
Matthew Bircham (13)	14
Molly Austen (13)	14
Helena Lewis (14)	15
Kate Phoenix (12)	15

Beechwood College, Penarth
Owen Cooper (21)	16

Bishop of Llandaff CW High School, Cardiff
Samuel Yahia (12)	16
Patrick Johnson (12)	17
Nicholas Anderson Fowler (12)	18
Daniel Price (13)	19
Joelle Gorno (13)	20
Hanna Lewis-Jones (13)	21

Caereinion High School, Welshpool
  Alexander Worth (15)   22

Cardiff High School, Cardiff
  Tomos Barry (14)   22
  Matthew Nicholls (14)   23
  Rhys Polley (15)   23
  Daniel Drummond (15)   24
  Peter Davies (15)   24
  Sophie Baggott (14)   25
  Lisa Carr (14)   25
  Sadia Zaman (15)   26
  Stephanie Emezie (15)   26
  Ana Vujanic (15)   27
  Caitlin Davies (14)   27
  Zoë Gallamore (14)   28
  Hollie Goman (15)   28
  Anwen Hayward (16)   29
  Emma Vincent Miller (14)   29
  Rosie Field (16)   30
  Jezel Jones (16)   30
  Babongile Ndiweni (16)   31
  Khadija Jamal (16)   31
  Tom Williams (16)   32
  Will Ashton (16)   32
  Laura Trigg (12)   33
  Rhian Evans (16)   33
  Sarah Vinestock (13)   34
  David Lloyd-Williams (16)   34
  Fahim Khan (12)   35
  Carolyn Sullivan (16)   35
  Jonathan Davies (12)   36
  Joseph Nichols (14)   36
  Bethan Ayres (12)   37
  Helen Nicholls (14)   37
  Rose Elinor Malleson (14)   38
  Hattie Clarke (17)   38
  Madeleine Chapman (14)   39

James Sully (13)	39
Daniel Nicol (14)	40
Daniela Salgado Silva (15)	40
Owen Thomas (15)	41
Claire Hodges (14)	41
Bethan Andrews (14)	41
Emily Marr (12)	42
Jack Narbed (15)	43
Ben Guan (15)	44
Alex Burns (15)	44
George Phillips (14)	45
Richard Warren (15)	45
Barnaby Pathy (14)	46
Jack Williams (14)	46
Alexander Marr (15)	47
Elliot Stockford (14)	47
Megan Evans (12)	48
Kian Maheri (15)	48
Dylan Johns (12)	49
Tom Hatch (15)	49
Jessica Schwartz (12)	50
Joel Gordon (12)	51
Elin Barrett (13)	51
Georgina Davies (12)	52
Harriet Averill (13)	53
Bryony Anderson (13)	54
Katherine Thomas (14)	55
Joshua Moore (15)	55
Daniel Bright (17)	56
Sarah Lovell (17)	57
Michael Dunn (15)	58
Maha Naeem (13)	58
Yousaf Jamal	59
Tabitha Kearney (12)	59
Luke James (17)	60
Peter Lloyd-Williams (12)	61
James Grace (14)	62

Denbigh High School, Denbigh

Jake Rooney (13)	62
Stephanie Farley (13)	63
Lisa Davies (13)	63
Ben Lovell (13)	64
Liam Rowlands (14)	65
Chelsea Wynne (14)	66
Ceri Jones (13)	67
Ella Richards (13)	68
Robert Jones (13)	68
Dion Lloyd-Williams (14)	69

Dyffryn Comprehensive School, Port Talbot

Sarah Rees (11)	69
Jacob Davies (12)	70
Lois Samuel (11)	71
Charli Davies (12)	71

Elfed High School, Buckley

Jamie Hewitt (14)	72
Rhian Taylor (14)	72
Kate Openshaw (15)	73
Katy Healing (15)	73
Ashleigh Boyle (14)	74
Caia Stevenson (15)	75
Richard Williams (14)	76
Sean Hughes (15)	77
Luke Webster (14)	78
Jake Anglesey (14)	79
Siân Evans (15)	79
Samantha Shaw (15)	80
Samantha Hird (15)	81

Hawarden High School, Hawarden

Laura Martin (13)	81
Leah Edwards (13)	82
Megan Brooke-Jones (11)	83
Eleanor Anne Wyndham Badhams (13)	84
Polly Mewse (12)	84

Kathryn Wakley (12)	85
Jessica Bennett (12)	85
Bethan Snowden-Jones (12)	86
Sophie-Lynne Williams (13)	87
Shannon Brooks (13)	88
Joe Turner (12)	89
Samantha Lawson (11)	90
Chelsie Davies (12)	91
Sarah Stachowski (12)	91
Kelly Evans (11)	92
Caitlin Taylor (11)	92
Sophie Evans (12)	93
Bryony Stark (13)	94
Jessie St Clair (13)	95
Bethany Evans (12)	96
Sara Perrett (12)	97
Lucy Birchall (11)	97
Daniel Williams (13)	98
Polly Greaves (12)	99
Amy Bingham (12)	99
Danielle Kaye (12)	100
Liam Ross (13)	101

Ysgol Bryn Elian, Old Colwyn

Chloe Mancini (14)	102
Samuel Walker (12)	103
Geena Watson (13)	103
Charlotte Stephenson (12)	104
Hollie Higgins (13)	105
Anna Wilson (14)	106
Mathew Roberts (14)	107
Ashleigh Steinson (14)	108
Jessica Simonds (14)	109
Max Smith (14)	109
Katy Williams (13)	110
Laura Rickard (14)	111
Josh Monaghan (14)	112
Lewis Roberts (13)	113
Katie Gough (13)	114

Abbie Wilson (13)	115
Katherine Barnes (14)	116
Natalie Hughes (14)	117
Charlotte Burgess (13)	118
Conner Bellwood (12)	119
Leila Edwards (11)	120
Ross Thorpe (11)	120
Calum Ryan (12)	121
Kayleigh Harris (12)	121
Thomas Walsh (13)	122
Eleri Evans (11)	123
Kora Hardern-Riley (13)	124
Jack Williams (13)	125
Steven Jones (13)	126
Dominik Fidor (13)	126
James Davies (12)	127
Amy Miller (11)	127
Daniel Thomas (13)	128
Sadie Boughen (11)	129
Bethany Ellis (13)	130
Toby Whitehead (14)	131
Danielle Louise Beddow (12)	132
Kayleigh Lewis (13)	133
Keeley Trow (12)	133
Sarah Wynne-Williams (12)	134
David Parry (12)	134
Lucy Jones (12)	135
Joseph Rickard (12)	135
Corrin Treleaven-Westwood (12)	136
Courtney Giblin (13)	137
Caitlin Baxter (11)	138
Jade Louise Griffiths (12)	138
Denzel Simon (14)	139
Alec Jones (12)	139
Chloe Mangnall (11)	140
Connor Nichols (12)	140
Bethany Starr (11)	141
Darren Arthur (12)	141
Tristan Rowllings (13)	142
Edward John Roberts (13)	143

Robert Richards (13)   144
Kyle Heath (12)   145
Tomos Williams (13)   146
Holly Griffith (13)   146
Stephen Toseland (12)   147
Kelly Anne Marsden (11)   147
Samantha Farah (12)   148
Natalie Hughes (12)   148
Phillip Roberts (12)   149
Ashley Holden (11)   149
Callum Hughes (13)   150
Chris Fowler (14)   150
Steph Dennis (14)   151
Ellesse Lauren Lynch (12)   151
Heidi Leanne Ellis (13)   152
Nicholas Ledden (12)   153
Glen Urquhart (12)   153

The Poems

Talking About My Generation

Pop stars and heroes taking drugs,
young kids turning into thugs.
People dying for making a stand.
What is becoming of our land?

Houses we won't be able to afford,
too many coming from abroad.
High fuel prices and even food,
so many of us in a bad mood.

Loud music and alco pops,
hanging on corners and bus stops,
old people afraid to walk by
staying in their homes without even a try.

Too many cars filling our concrete roads
aeroplanes and lorries all adding to the load.
The ozone layer is getting so thin,
pollution is killing this world we live in.

We are the generation to start anew,
respect our elders is what we must do.
Switch off the lights and start to walk,
listen to each other when we start to talk.

Say *no* to drugs and *no* to drink,
before we speak we must learn to think,
tell on the bullies, don't be afraid
and stand up for all the new friends you have made.

Harry Varney (12)
Alun School, Mold

What You've Done To Me

My skin slowly began to bruise,
As my heart slowly began to break,
You began to destroy me as the time went on,
So I hope you're proud of what you've done to me.

You hurt me not only on the outside,
You also hurt deep inside of me,
My heart was falling apart into tiny pieces,
As you began to win the prize that you've always wanted.

The whole time you thought I was in the wrong,
But really you are for doing something so uncaring,
God would've helped you with your problems,
You could have just left me alone but now it's too late.

Every time I see someone I begin to get scared,
I used to feel like I had someone pulling me back,
When I want to go forwards you just won't let go,
Part of me will never trust again now.

Remi Whelan (13)
Alun School, Mold

My Generation

Drugs, guns and violence,
Outside the local off-licence,
You pop inside Bargain Booze
And you leave with a big brown bruise.

Afghanistan and Iraq war,
Need I say no more,
Dead or alive,
My generation needs to make peace.

Children silenced at Haut de la Garenne,
Secrets still to be uncovered,
DNA and bodies need to be uncovered,
My generation - the truth at last.

Kieren Turner Owen (12)
Alun School, Mold

My Generation

Many adults say our youth is going wrong,
That gun crime and rape are a common thing,
That people get mugged because they're different,
That reality TV shows are shaping our minds,
That fame and fortune is all we want,
Knife attacks, smoking, drinking is all we do.
Why don't you realise this is a minority?
That most of us are hardworking and respectful?
That we will grow up to correct your mistakes?
Major decisions are coming our way,
That will shape the future of mankind,
That will save the world or help destroy it.
So give us support and teach all you know,
Help us to win the war we will face,
Help get rid of the minority that people will remember.
Help save the world from chaos.

James Grundy (13)
Alun School, Mold

What's Happened To Me?

When I was younger
I wanted to be a captain sailing the sea,
A pirate, a fireman, everything that came to me.
In my sunny childhood before 9/11 and 7/7
And these images no child should see,
It affected everyone around the world including me
When I grow up now I want to be a soldier
In Iraq, in Afghanistan fighting the enemy.
What's happened to me?

Nicholas Roberts (12)
Alun School, Mold

My Generation

Meeting mates,
Hanging out,
Late nights,
Having fun.

Creme Eggs, Red Bull, cheese on toast
I've only just begun.

Birthdays,
Christmas,
Having money,
Chester on the bus.

Holidays; there aren't enough!
But I won't create a fuss.

Cos I've got
Summertime in the park,
Catchy songs,
Playing footie.

Ice cream vans and lemonade,
Camping out with my best mates.

But . . .
Early mornings,
Dark and dreary,
School uniform,
Mondays.

Sprouts and bedtime, Jamie's dinners,
Enough to turn us all into sinners.

Parents nagging,
Being skint,
Having no cred,
Not so mint!

All in all it's not so bad,
I'm better looking then my dad!

Gareth Thomas (13)
Alun School, Mold

Down To Earth

Our generation's changed quite a lot these days,
Drugs and gangsters all society has changed.
People think life's so unfair,
But do they look in the open air,
Where there's wars and violence, poverty too,
What is the world going to do?
Families splitting but health is better,
Now the computer instead of a letter.

Forest of trees cut down for pleasure,
Animals slaughtered for our own leisure.
Why is the world now a horrible place,
Where people get injured because of their race.
The world really needs to change,
Or global warming might end our days.

Sophie Greatbatch (12)
Alun School, Mold

Gadgets

Everyone has an iPod or mp3 player
They all have Sky or Freeview on a big TV
Some are flat and others are fat
Don't forget the PSP, 2, 3
The special features on DVD
Faster Internet on the PC
Better mobile phones with music players and 30 cameras
Lots of things are better in my generation.

Beth Lloyd (14)
Alun School, Mold

My Generation

Terror sets off a shock
9/11 so painful to watch
What is happening to us
Our generation
Immune from horror
We could all be gone tomorrow.

Every day kids go missing, found dead
Watching the misery, nothing to be said
What is happening to us
Our generation
Immune from murder
We cannot sink any further.

President Bush as large as life
His face fills the screen
His words predict strife
What is happening to us
Our generation
Get the big guns
What will be the future of our sons?

In our world there are places of peace filled with love
To be found within our friends and families
Who do not judge
What will happen to us
Our generation
We will survive and go on
With determination, hope and a war-free zone.

Kristina Waxler (13)
Alun School, Mold

Talkin' 'Bout My Generation

There's a plane flying by
A car speeding, oh my
Cold weather today
Hot weather yesterday
Pollution can never stay away.

Football, music, meditation
Talkin' 'bout my generation
Houses all over the place
People with a plastic face
Living costs are going up
Population is on the up
Yet there are still differences between race.

Football, music, meditation
Talkin' 'bout my generation
Computers complete with Internet
On which people can place a bet
Racism and drugs
It's all done by thugs
Why are people always in debt?

Football, music, meditation
Talkin' 'bout my generation
Football, music, meditation
Talkin' 'bout *my* generation!

Luke Van Der Kooij (12)
Alun School, Mold

My Generation

Will mobile phones help mend broken bones?
Will HDTV stop poverty?
Will watching Ronaldo hit the net eradicate global debt?
No.

My generation only care about popularity
Buying the new gadgets instead of giving to charity.
Wanting more and more
Not feeling grateful for what they have got.
Pretending there's no such thing as poor,
Until a repo man kicks them out the door.

But to look on the bright side of things
We're better at recycling
And we don't spend as much time talking
So why do the adults make a fuss
When they're the ones kidnapping us?
And although we may commit more crimes
At least we can write a poem that rhymes.

Cameron Leiper (13)
Alun School, Mold

Drugs

D rugs in my generation.
R eckon you're hard but you're *not*.
U sing them damages your health.
G oing high makes you feel invincible
   when you are most vulnerable.
S illy boys and girls die every year from *drug* abuse.

Ben Szulc (13)
Alun School, Mold

War

Two little sisters stand in what once was a street
Rubble all around their bare feet
They cry out for help
But no one can hear their voices
They are orphans with no choice.

Bodies and blood are scattered around
As they slowly walk on the rough ground
Their family and friends lie in pools of blood
But how can they know what's going on
As they are only little ones.

Their eyes well up with tears
As their memories are tied up with fears
They will never forget this day
As their lives have changed forever
Telling the same tragic story of the war to one another.

This is our generation so what will be next?
More war, more blood or more deaths
Let's not make this happen for our future children's sake
And make this world a better place.

Molly Reid (13)
Alun School, Mold

My Generation

In my generation there is new technology
Lots of people study astronomy
There is a bit more racism
But there's a lot more terrorism
Buy a gun, make some violence
Buy some cigarettes from the off-licence
Some people think it's a good generation
Some people think it isn't in our nation.

Stefan Rosier (13)
Alun School, Mold

My Generation

Some people say, my generation is the best,
Others say it is the worst.
My generation is the future.
Technology, where would we be without it?
When adults were kids some things didn't exist
That today we take for granted.
Everyone has a mobile phone to communicate all the time,
If you're going to be late, you can call your mate
And rearrange your time.
This was not the case years ago, if you couldn't make it
Your friend would just have to wait
And think that you were a bad mate.
The first computers were so big, they filled an entire house,
These days you can buy computers
That are just as small as a mouse.
Going on holiday is the best,
You have the time of your life,
But when you come home everything is a blur
And you are back to your normal everyday life.
People wear what they feel comfortable in,
You can tell someone's personality by the way they dress.
But if you wear an old granny skirt
You will be kicked around like a piece of dirt.

Charlotte Hewitt (14)
Alun School, Mold

My Generation

Smiles once roamed free everywhere I looked
Time changed . . .
Buildings and homes came crumbling down
Innocent people's lives got taken
Tears, cries and grief surrounded me.

Islands, trees and extraordinary animals once owned our world
Time changed . . .
Sea levels raised, undiscovered animals became extinct
Our homes soon will be underwater
There is no harm in sharing our home with nature.

Intelligence invented TVs but never thought of its consequence
Time changed . . .
Children became addicted to TVs
They became overweight
Children wasted their lives watching TV.

People once lived in peace and harmony
Time changed . . .
People fought and murdered over money
Selfishness and greed was shown in the eyes of everyone
Money brought everything but never love or happiness.

Anokhi Patel (13)
Alun School, Mold

Generation

What kind of generation is this?
This generation I call my own
Where even a young child
Is afraid to go home
Now their lives lived in fear
Their hormones going wild
What kind of generation is this?
This generation I call my own
A generation so full of lies
Can you spot the liars?
Can you see it in their eyes?
A generation where self expression
Is pushed and made to fall
Despised and destroyed
To boast the egos of them all
A generation where bombs blow up
A generation where racism grows strong
A generation that makes you go crazy
A generation that's without morals
A generation that's without shame
A generation that seems so dark
A generation that seems so cold
A generation that kills the young
A generation that scars the old
But underneath all that bad
Lays some good you see
Like technology and different things
And people who can sing
We take for granted everything
And don't say thank you or please
We watch television nearly every day
We don't even have to wash anymore
This kind of generation is my own
Music has changed just as much
From being the same to being unique
This kind of generation
Is my own so that is why I call it . . .
My generation.

Ffion Rowlands (14)
Alun School, Mold

My Generation

In the 60s
They said words like nifty
And how much money
Was a fifty!

But our language has changed
We have our own phone
With clothes, hair and words.

In the 60s
Rebellion was rife
But rebels now
Is everyday life.

Tootie frootie
Apple pie
Sherbet dips
And fatty thighs.

Clever scientists
Read the sky
New inventions every day
More amazing in every way.

Listened to parents
Did as they said
If not, they would be sent to bed.

New animals
But dying out
Rainforest falling
Without a doubt.

Julia Bond (14)
Alun School, Mold

Our Generation

Our generation's all about new technology,
Breakthroughs in astronomy and astrology.
Fashion changing all the time
And many different types of crime.
We've got racism, we've got terrorism,
The media fill us in on the television.
We couldn't wait for the millennium and then it came,
There will never be celebrations the same.
Children with their mobile phones and mp3s,
With all the fast food, so many people are obese.
Anti-social behaviour is on the rise,
Football's the most important thing in most children's eyes.
People going round driving motorbikes and cars,
Overflowing prisons, because of too many being put behind bars.
People walking round the streets, talking in slang,
They have to talk like that though, just to be part of the gang.
These things are happening all across the nation,
I'm just talkin' 'bout my generation.

Matthew Bircham (13)
Alun School, Mold

Dying Generation

G eneration, how many more will there be?
E nergy falling as fast as a cut tree.
N o more laughter, no more play,
E veryone's just taking this away.
R ound and round the Earth it spins,
A nd if people would just use the bins!
T ick-tock, listen to the clock,
I nnocent time is running amok.
O pen air is running low.
N ow please people, don't say no!

Molly Austen (13)
Alun School, Mold

Class 4E Visit The Zoo

On the bus Class 4E waited in excitement,
The colours of lunch boxes, coats and bags filled each row,
After tedious registers and checks off they went.

Out of the windows Timmy and Poppy
Looked at the cities and the several streams,
But most of the children were away in their dreams.

After half an hour the bus stopped
Which was followed by a thud
Because Bobbie's lunch box had dropped.

They met all the animals one by one
And then all the class stopped at the picnic area
For lunch and a scone.

Overall the class liked the monkey the best
Because a lot of the animals were having a rest.

They visited the gift shop and Poppy bought a yo-yo
But then the class had to go.

All the class had homework to do
But in their minds they were still at the zoo.

Helena Lewis (14)
Alun School, Mold

Music

Music, there are so many different types,
from rock and pop, dance to hip hop.
Solo songs from the heart and songs
that hit the top of the chart.
Cheesy songs that my mum knows,
they make me want to wriggle my toes.
Beatbox, rapping all night long,
I really do love all of these songs.

Kate Phoenix (12)
Alun School, Mold

Twenty First Century Plague

My friends bleed from thy testament's greed;
the slaughtered saints of disease's creed,
the successors of the fallen in lead.
Seek I a final whisper of life,
a reconciliation against this strife;
the homeless gather along the trail of the knife,
their numbers spiralling to unimaginable rife.
Yet no law there is that is writ,
extends to us as is fit;
degraded are those that are bit,
re-amputated or reduced to . . .
Fresh faces gloat with evil eyes,
under the parasol of the night sky;
soon I shall cry goodbye, but with relief that's no lie.

Owen Cooper (21)
Beechwood College, Penarth

The Environment

Getting worse and worse,
Day in, day out.
How can we stop it?
If we even try the government will only shout.

So much CO_2 in the atmosphere,
We need to find an alternative right now, right here.
The greenhouse effect making the Earth get hotter and hotter,
Who do we need? A Harry Potter.

And as for the ozone layer,
Getting thinner and thinner.
But yet slowly and slowly and slowly,
The Earth begins to simmer.

The precious fossil fuels of the Earth,
Running out faster than ever,
And to add to that,
The way we use them is not clever.

Samuel Yahia (12)
Bishop of Llandaff CW High School, Cardiff

My Generation - Some Kind Of Joke?

My generation, a bunch of idiots?
Vandalism, racism, cynicism
Every day on the news, Britain's youth out of control
What else is new?

Are we all bad?
Do you ever hear anything good my generation has achieved?
I'm sure there are some things
Only time will tell.

We like, what we like
Nothing more nothing less
It's our thing
Stop trying to force your interests on us.

School is a laugh
Friends can be mad
Always up to something
You never know with them.

It's great when the weekend comes
Plenty to do
Hardly enough time
Things speed up.

And I've come to the end of the page it seems
That's the rules, one A4 side
No longer than thirty lines
Wait, that's not enough!

Patrick Johnson (12)
Bishop of Llandaff CW High School, Cardiff

Just About Getting Over It

Here he comes in his large hooded coat,
Scaring away all the townsfolk
Who will he take today?

Wildly swinging his big heavy scythe,
People trying to send him away with their small and puny knives,
They are no match for him.

People trying to send him away but he's not going empty-handed.
Wizards and witches join the fight,
Sending huge blasts of light.

Nobody at all wants to leave their friends and family behind,
One person has got to go
And make the daunting sacrifice.

That man over there looks at me, I shake my head,
In return, he can't go, no he can't
He's heading over to death.

That's me over there in the corner crying and whinging away,
My grandfather, gone in a few seconds.
My world has come to nothing.

My world has gone . . . nothing matters now,
My best friend vanished into Heaven.

He's always watching over us, he's here all the time,
Let's just get on in life.

Nicholas Anderson Fowler (12)
Bishop of Llandaff CW High School, Cardiff

Talkin' 'Bout My Generation

Not so much happening these days
But there are things happening in more than one way.
People are in public schools
Being bullied, and made to look like fools.

Sam, I am using a 'fake' name
But people are driving him insane.
Bullying is such a horrid thing
So why are people doing it, bullying?

Poor old Sam, scared to go to school,
I don't blame him, his friends ain't cool.
As soon as he gets there somebody says,
'Oi Sam, give me your money, I need my pay.'

So this is it, talking about my generation,
It's not a great deal, it's not a lot of fun,
It's quite a bore, and I have a fear
Of going to school, which I try not to shed a tear.

Above all, I have a great fear,
What'll happen to me now and here.
Well, I'd wish to hurry up and die
So, here I am, ready to commit suicide.

Daniel Price (13)
Bishop of Llandaff CW High School, Cardiff

And Some In-Between

There are people everywhere you go
In the corridor and in the hall
There are girls and boys
And just some in-between
You've got nice teachers and mean teachers
And some in-between
There are emos and wannabes
And some in-between
There are smelly boys and weird boys
And some in-between
There are girly girls and moody girls
And some in-between

Wherever you go
Someone wants to know
Who that girl just kissed
Or why he deserved a fist.

Joelle Gorno (13)
Bishop of Llandaff CW High School, Cardiff

My Generation

Ravenous children,
Forced by hunger
To labour and to toil,
Long days from dawn until dusk.

Long hours,
Low wages,
Sweated labour with
No protection from abuse.

Grinding poverty
Of the Third World.
Giving cheap clothing,
To us at a cost.

Young lives cut short
Below the poverty line.

Hanna Lewis-Jones (13)
Bishop of Llandaff CW High School, Cardiff

A Thousand Words

A thousand words will never say
How much I miss you every day.
A thousand words will never show
How much it is I love you so.

As we go through the winter chill
And I talk to you, my happy pill,
If there's one thing you have made me decide,
It's that I need you here by my side.

A thousand words will never fear,
A solemn life without you here,
A thousand words will never care
That without you I am stripped bare.

The fire I feel spreading through me
Burns into my soul, setting me free,
Melting my whole heart with a look,
Proves it's you I love, and darling, I'm hooked.

Alexander Worth (15)
Caereinion High School, Welshpool

Nightmare

Screams sound high as night approaches
And a smell of death fills the air.
Another wounded soul drags a shattered body,

Blackened and bruised, no chance of survival.
I lay him to rest and shut his eyes.
Another man gone whose eyes see no more

Light, no warmth or joy or bliss.
Screams sound high as day approaches
But the smell of death remains.

Tomos Barry (14)
Cardiff High School, Cardiff

Loss

They came at midnight,
The air thick and humid.
The barren desert was filled
With the echoing cries
Of crickets and alarming
Regular screams.

The youthful child lies
On the firm desert floor,
Her body twisted and jagged
In impossible angles
With a trail of blood
Connecting her body
To the wooden hut.

They had come again.

Matthew Nicholls (14)
Cardiff High School, Cardiff

Take A Bow

    It builds
With power and passion,
    Pulse and pace,
The ecstasy pulsates
    From this vibe.
The leader stands
    Before the creator
Hands waving, guiding
      Success -
    Take a bow.

Rhys Polley (15)
Cardiff High School, Cardiff

Rainy Afternoons

Let me show you the past,
When all the knowledge of man
Was stored in snow-white pages like these,
And hidden away in leather bound tombs.

Fact and fiction,
Written down in hope of it,
Enduring time's ravages and surviving,
Trapped in yellowing, dog-eared pages.

Let me show you the past,
Where knowledge was power
And power was everything.
Let me show you the ancient past.

It was called a book.

Daniel Drummond (15)
Cardiff High School, Cardiff

La Luna

The moon is like a smile from space,
Like a clown's never-ending smirk.
The moon is a nocturnal sun
Like a dreamer waking in the night.

The skies are lit by the crystal moon,
A parallel sun glowing in the dark.
A silver pebble splashed out onto the sky
Like a ping-pong ball bouncing around the Earth.

It grows and shrinks, waxes and wanes
Now covered by the tissue paper of cloud.
Its facial expression bursts out
With a wink it lights up the heavens.

Peter Davies (15)
Cardiff High School, Cardiff

The Owl

The night beckons with its crooked finger
As the sun gives out the last of its rays.
I descend from the hollow oak tree
Where I spend my lonely days.

The noise from the underground rattles
And it's impossible to turn a deaf ear.
Sometimes I pretend otherwise
But there is nothing I don't hear.

My wisdom is known throughout the wood.
From day to day I wait in my tree,
Ready for questions posed by smaller birds
Though good answers are not guaranteed.

Sophie Baggott (14)
Cardiff High School, Cardiff

The Moon

The moon is a pure white cat prowling the inky night
And its pawprints leave a magic trail
Which glows in the ebony sky.
It is a glistening bauble that sways in the wind,
A milky white button nibbled by hungry stars.
The moon is every child's comforting refuge
And a gleaming white jewel engraved
In an opaque, black surface.
Bright as a diamond that glimmers
In the midnight sky, a glowing night light
Promising reassurance you are not alone.

Lisa Carr (14)
Cardiff High School, Cardiff

Dream

She fell through the sky, a fallen angel,
Into the misty land of surreality.
The immense valley created a shroud
Of demented dreams.
She couldn't fall apart at the seams.
She could put her mind against herself,
Twisted by imagination.
He had an acidic tongue,
Changing her thoughts, so frail and young.
A grimace played at his lips.
She turned away,
Afraid.
What creature is imagination?
Where does he lurk?
Only she knows,
It's all inside her head . . .

Sadia Zaman (15)
Cardiff High School, Cardiff

My Place In The Scheme Of Things

Twilight ends the day
Now comes the cover of dark
Rapidly it spreads
Sucking the light from the stars
Are my eyes even open?

Stephanie Emezie (15)
Cardiff High School, Cardiff

Reverse

Outside in the cold,
Throwing out the big black bags,
I race down the stairs
After using up twenty-three tissue boxes.
Slumped on the bed,
With a colossal ache in the head,
Heart left discarded on the floor,
I hang up the phone
And listen to the harsh, ruthless tone.
Rolling down my flustered cheek
Tears prick my eyes.
I answer with equal coolness.
I recognise your voice,
Picking up the handle
I answer the phone.

Ana Vujanic (15)
Cardiff High School, Cardiff

Search For Identity

A jumble of thoughts
Mixed and messed up. So confused
Dreams. Ripped at the seams
Missing jigsaw piece
Does anyone know the truth?

Caitlin Davies (14)
Cardiff High School, Cardiff

Love

Like a river that flows eternal,
Like a flower that blooms in the spring,
Like hope that rises to meet the lengthening gloom,
Love will carry on.

Courage as deep as despair,
Ice as sharp as fire,
Silence as heavy as sound,
Love will carry on.

Sun, moon, star,
Light, dark, twilight,
Black, white, grey,
Love will carry on.

Like a river that flows eternal,
Ice as sharp as fire,
Black, white, grey,
Love surpasses all.

Zoë Gallamore (14)
Cardiff High School, Cardiff

Illusory World

Hold your breath and jump
Let go of your fantasy
Careful, watch your step
Whispers of humanity
A colourful illusion.

Hollie Goman (15)
Cardiff High School, Cardiff

Serenity

The words spring to life
As if they were free
On page twenty-nine.

I uncheck the adjectives
Leave in 'nice' and 'good'
And put unnecessary words back in.

Erase all the images
That my mind's eye will never see
And the unwanted ink seeps through.

Rinse off the similies
Delete the metaphors
And sweep mist over the adverbs.

Finally
I put down my pen
And I have finished.

Anwen Hayward (16)
Cardiff High School, Cardiff

Butterfly

Breezily, effortless
Wings delicate like snowflakes
Fluttering, weightless
Tiny in the sea of blue
Immense in terms of beauty.

Emma Vincent Miller (14)
Cardiff High School, Cardiff

Through The Glass

Staring at you through the glass.
Don't know how much time has passed.
I look at you with much despair
To stare at something so beautiful,
So elegant, so fair.

I fight the temptation to touch you
To feel your ghostly presence,
The walls in which I'm breathing
My mind is un-weaving.

How can you exist in my world?
This place of imperfection.
I know that you will save me
From all of the obscene.

Rosie Field (16)
Cardiff High School, Cardiff

Without A Sound

A high-pitched note
Sung with a shaking wrist,
A softly sliding bow.

My chin tilted slightly,
Violin resting on a chunky sponge
Resin dust on the floor.

A flat note plucked.
Out of its silk cover it slides,
Zip undone with care.

Reaching for the highest shelf,
A dusty, forgotten case I see.
Still, without a sound.

Jezel Jones (16)
Cardiff High School, Cardiff

Once It Was

Once it was a home
In the hot African sun
Shadowed by crescent moons.

Once it was a tunnel
Filled with passages of delight
Where snakes lingered.

Once it was a pod
So sweet and wet that
Eggshells dared not touch.

But now it is a memory
Of pleasure and of pain
And the aroma keeps you.

Babongile Ndiweni (16)
Cardiff High School, Cardiff

School Boredom Syndrome

Every two metres across the class
And every so often, out of nowhere
I see them, bobbing up and down
Tiny models of castles
You know, just sort of
Floating about in the air.

Khadija Jamal (16)
Cardiff High School, Cardiff

Bermuda's Square

I met a traveller, who'd told me he'd seen,
The apple in my eye wiped clean.

He said he'd seen where man once stood,
A place now strewn with rotten wood.

Razed to dust; the King's estranged,
'A timeless place' - this meaning changed.

He said he'd seen where light once shone,
But over now, it's all but gone.

A garden once, the seeds were sewn,
But where they lay, is still unknown.

A country's pride was there at high,
But knocked back down when the time was nigh.

A lesson taught? Who's there to say?
Keep to the path - don't go astray.

The time will come to meet thy fear,
Play it safe, keep your conscience clear.

So there he stood, Bermuda's Square,
But where'd it go? There's nothing there!

Tom Williams (16)
Cardiff High School, Cardiff

Me

A basking shark, thoughtful and drifting.
The gardens of Babylon, mysterious and beyond reach.
Extreme ironing, pointless but fun.
A mongrel, smarter than a pedigree.
Influenza, annoying and persistent.
Dopey, friendly, but misunderstood.

Will Ashton (16)
Cardiff High School, Cardiff

My Wales

A busy, noisy, congested city,
Houses ten to a penny,
Some parkland, few fields, a glistening lake,
Bustling, rowdy, never alone,
This is my home!

Rolling hills, shimmering rivers, no pollution,
No traffic, houses few and far between,
A couple of villages, widely spread out,
Tranquil, calm, but not lonely,
This is my nana's and Taid's home!

White sand, crashing waves,
Caravans above the dunes,
Mountains, clear on the horizon,
Peaceful, quiet, time to relax.
This is my caravan!

This is my Wales!

Laura Trigg (12)
Cardiff High School, Cardiff

On My List

A curious sparrow flitting along the cerulean skies,
Hop-stepping softly across cracked grey,

Bubbly ruby cherryade fizzing away innocently,
Impatiently waiting to explode in a foamy burst,

A unique language known not even to me,
But at least I know what I'm saying,

That happy old dwarf with the wizened eyes,
Chubby dimples a picture of cheer.

Rhian Evans (16)
Cardiff High School, Cardiff

Our World

Trekking through the vast desert,
no water, no life
Trekking through the hot, vast desert,
no water, food, no life
Trekking through the golden, hot, vast desert,
no water, no life
This is not our world.

Hiking up the massive Mount Everest,
no sun, no life
Hiking up the terrifying, massive Mount Everest,
no sun, warmth, no life
This is not our world.

Strolling in the peaceful Welsh countryside,
plenty of water and life
The cows and sheep grazing
The pigs bathing in mud
Strolling in the luscious, peaceful Welsh countryside,
plenty of water, sun and life.
The daffodils popping out
Blossoming in the green fields
This is our world . . .
This is Wales!

Sarah Vinestock (13)
Cardiff High School, Cardiff

Church Bells

A bluebird flying high on wings of a song,
A Welsh voice raised high, Harlech passion strong,

A burning sun shining so wide and so bright,
A golden dog leading those without sight,

And in my heart Barcelona's where I belong,
Church bells in my soul are urging me on.

David Lloyd-Williams (16)
Cardiff High School, Cardiff

War Bombs

Bombs, every second of fear and stress,
worried sick of gas or a mustard bomb
suffocating you to death.
Every moment you walk you feel the fear.

Scared wherever you go,
You may be killed one place and left there to suffer,
Cruelty wherever you walk,
'Run boys! Mustard bombs!'
Boom! exploded one, and then another.
Twenty friends as a group; bombs hit us, ten came out alive.

The smell of war was intense,
The smell of corpses rotting like a fruit,
And the smell of unwashed soldiers stinking of BO.

They saw corpses lying there staring at them,
Faces full of guilt,
Every spirit haunting them as they fought.

Fahim Khan (12)
Cardiff High School, Cardiff

Let Me Tell You

When the moon rises to the sky
And my eyelids fall
Reality emerges soon to die.
My personality changes
Strangers stroll through my mind
I'm a demon of evil
Bubble of fright, tornado of bliss
In a panic that the sun will rise
And the night forces will miss.

Carolyn Sullivan (16)
Cardiff High School, Cardiff

Rat-A-Tat, Swoosh, Boom, Bang!

Rat-a-tat, swoosh, boom, bang!
The noises echoed again and again
Going on forever as time itself
Disappeared
Constantly guns fired
And after every bullet a life was to be lost.

Squelching through the trenches
My feet, damp, smelly, tired
Looking at the dead bodies
Rotting away
The men who died, died as heroes
Rat-a-tat, swoosh, boom, bang!

In the foggy-filled sky, planes competed
Bombs dropped, exploding sadness
In every corner
Smoke surrounding the air with a blanket of gas
Covering screaming voices of scared soldiers

Rat-a-tat, swoosh, boom, bang!
My friend, you would not tell with such high zest
To children, ardent for some desperate glory,
The old lie: *Dulce et decorum est*
Pro patria mori.

Jonathan Davies (12)
Cardiff High School, Cardiff

Ugly Sister

I climb the thirty steps to my room
To seek the adventure that lurks there.
The violin, cornet and three-piece band
Play heavy songs in my ears.

Since I am not bewitched in adolescence
I will retreat to trees and gracious silence
And to the wind that does not make movement.

Joseph Nichols (14)
Cardiff High School, Cardiff

My War Poem

Soldiers lying on the ground
The sound of gunshot all around
Black, black smoke drifts across the sky
The look of fear in their eye

Mustard gas filling the air
They're praying for their mother's care
To my home I long to go
My wife and child, I love you so

The smell of death fills my mind
I've lost my faith in human kind
Strong wind blowing from the south
The poisoned gas burns my mouth

Bombs like fireworks in the sky
Please my God don't let me die
I try to think of days gone by
Not of where my dead friends lie

I want to go back to my life
I really want to see my wife
I want to see my child once more
And never fight another war.

Bethan Ayres (12)
Cardiff High School, Cardiff

Inner Sight

She lays inside herself
Listening to the world around
Her eyes like open doors
A passage into her dreamworld
To see spirit deep within.

Helen Nicholls (14)
Cardiff High School, Cardiff

The Sea

The sea is as cold as fresh snow,
That burns your fingers with smatters of ice.
It slithers like a snake, twisting, turning
Exploiting weakness in the coastal wall.

The sea sends in cavalry on white horses
Smashing into droplets unable to leave
Their watery homes, masking in lonely
Colours, hiding exotic lands:
Sometimes striking azure-blue
Sometimes stormy steel and grey.

The sea sways beneath the stars
Like two lovers dancing through night.

Rose Elinor Malleson (14)
Cardiff High School, Cardiff

The Galley Door

One key for life
That will fit for eternity
Allowing no choice or freedom
Only the scraping of metal along my sides
A chain of repetitive turns.

But, when the key is removed
And this door left wide open
The wind rushes through me
And I dream of what it must be
To not be under lock and key.

Hattie Clarke (17)
Cardiff High School, Cardiff

Losing A Loved One

If I'd stayed up with you all night,
Then I'd know how to save life,
A ghostly complexion my eyes met upon,
A still figure fresh on the crumpled sheet,
Wide awake in a world of pure bliss,
Breath echoes through his body,
Full of life in a world of imagination,
A soft daze to appreciate
A vortex of unwinding thoughts,
A deathly kiss goodbye to loved ones,
A click of a button, a black picture on the screen.

Madeleine Chapman (14)
Cardiff High School, Cardiff

Flowing Fields

Time stops, fields flow, only one stands,
careful footsteps through the land of emerald giants.

They know I'm there but stand regardless,
looking onto the quiet corners with crystal silence.

I stop and think, there's nothing
all the worries of the world left behind to a distant memory.

Fate made it so that I would be forever lost in the gardens
of the palace of joyful peace.

James Sully (13)
Cardiff High School, Cardiff

Real Reading

Beyond the dry pages
Of adventure and triumph
Lies the real world
Bathed in poverty
And illness.

Human cargoes crammed into
Camps like sardines in a tin,
Diseases spreading like wild fire.

Is this what mankind is reduced to?

Mother Nature lies
In a hospital bed.

The rhythm of life stops

And man is held
At gunpoint.

Daniel Nicol (14)
Cardiff High School, Cardiff

Longing

Empty ambitions
Her hope dangles on a string
Pitiful craving
Closed to her mind's fantasy
Her desires become unreal.

Daniela Salgado Silva (15)
Cardiff High School, Cardiff

Cheetah

My black spots blur past you
With my immense pace
Quick enough to catch any prey.
My sharp claws cut you apart
With just one swipe,
Leaving you crying out
In pain, helpless on the floor.
My punch catches you
Out with surprise.

Although my name
Says one thing
Beware, I play fair.

Owen Thomas (15)
Cardiff High School, Cardiff

Creature Realm

Stars twinkle gently
The darkened night settles in
Animals whisper
Silky curtains of moonbeams
Reveal wondrous new worlds.

Claire Hodges (14)
Cardiff High School, Cardiff

Dream Country

Surreal nightmare
Daydreaming and delusion
Unreal, faraway
Lost in misty slumber
Until you wake up again.

Bethan Andrews (14)
Cardiff High School, Cardiff

The Magnificent Dragon

As spring draws near there is still a chill in the air,
The dragon awakes and emerges from his lair,
A dark cave carved in the mountain,
Apart from the rest of his kingdom,
Lost in the misty Welsh hills,
Surrounded by carpets of daffodils,
He stretches his aching limbs,
And unfolds his powerful wings,
He steps boldly onto the dewy ground,
To survey his mythical land,
And remembers what he once saw . . .

Tribes of Celts smelting metal ore,
Using handmade stone tools,
Druids gathering on the banks of sacred pools,
Forests of emerald-green pine trees,
Cloaking the deep valleys,
And later Arthur pulling the sword from the stone,
When no one was left but him alone,
The brave saint, David,
Who, in March, is celebrated,
By people all over the country,
Who sing and dance merrily.

The majestic dragon lifts his head,
His scales glowing crimson with the sun ahead,
Now the morning mist has lifted,
To reveal a sky so limpid,
And the peaceful valley below
Is preparing for the celebrations tomorrow,
When the treasured flag will rise,
Bearing the magnificent dragon as a prize.

Emily Marr (12)
Cardiff High School, Cardiff

Colours

A river of colour and music
Runs through a people-filled street,
Trumpets and trombones wail and shout
As people run and dance.

The carnival
Releases its joy
To the people
Who throw confetti
And sing from their balconies.

Into this celebration of life
Comes a man
A man of order and propriety
Clothed in the pinstriped uniform of his life.

Suddenly he is gripped by a longing
For freedom
He runs into the street
Singing and dancing
His pinstriped suit
No match for the colourful
Dresses of the parading women.

He has cast off the rules of his life.
He lives for the moment.

He throws his hat into the air
A bird
That flies over the city of colour.

Jack Narbed (15)
Cardiff High School, Cardiff

Darkness And Thunder

Darkness emerges from its presence of the mind,
Thunder crashes right through the sky,
Not a soul can be heard over the rushing waves,
Black, nothing.
All is lost.

Darkness sweeps from a head,
A man or two, lost in the swirling darkness,
Black, white, nothing is seen.
All is lost.

Swirling clouds fly from the mind,
Angels of the heavens,
Fly from the skies always circling the clouds,
All is lost.

An albatross springs out of the head,
Showing nothing, but only the blackness of a mind,
Darkness only follows,
All is lost.

The waters are swift to emerge from a mind,
Swift and chuckling,
A ship of black comes from the fog,
Sails flapping, darkness swirling,
All as to say, is lost,
Only to darkness.

Ben Guan (15)
Cardiff High School, Cardiff

Dream Line

Falling slowly, the
Flighty thoughts of a flighty mind
Soar to rescue
Dreamland's home of knightly sky
End ill-timed disturbances.

Alex Burns (15)
Cardiff High School, Cardiff

The Mind

In this world, is a world of destruction.
Twisted lines, of fear and panic,
The world falling into pieces,
By the over-running of creatures.

The dinosaur's tongue is lashing out,
Spiders are lurking in the mist of the mind,
Whales and sharks are scouting the ruins,
Of the damage of the chaos.

Stars and moons fill up the scattered sky,
Like vivid patterns soaring through the night sky.
Down below, mountains are being inhabited by monsters,
Hunting for petrified humans.

Terror is throughout the world,
Distressed people are to be seen everywhere.
There is no such silence in a world,
As this is no ordinary world.

That is why they call it the mind.

George Phillips (14)
Cardiff High School, Cardiff

The Stone

They ride the waves,
Under a perfect shining sun,
Speeding down the beach,
To their new destination,
They gather on the sand,
In a meeting of the tide,
Listening to their stories.

Richard Warren (15)
Cardiff High School, Cardiff

The Animal Man

Like a tiger, waiting to strike,
Like a rabbit, quick left, then quick right,
He's a rhino, a snake,
Beware, keep awake,
Like a waterfall, the wait is immense,
Will he run or maybe defence?
Like a river, he's calm,
Then suddenly alarm,
The beast inside is awoken,
Everything in his path is broken,
Curving through Carter,
Like a knife through butter,
Till the ball he stole,
At last, reaches its goal,
This is *rugby* at its best,
You will be impressed.

Barnaby Pathy (14)
Cardiff High School, Cardiff

Refugee Camp

The heat hits me flat in the face
As insects buzz around.
A sad old man mourns in the corner
While a boy reads his invisible book
In a place unsuitable for humans.

Jack Williams (14)
Cardiff High School, Cardiff

Pebble Rain

The wind rushes over the wild moor
Accompanied by heavy rain
A scant figure shuffles, I am not sure
From whence this old man came.

'Pebbles fall from aching sky . . . '
He hollers through the night
I am puzzled, cannot reply
My surprise soon turns to fright.

So when he fades into the dark
I think his words again
Do pebbles fall from aching skies
Or is it nought but rain?

Alexander Marr (15)
Cardiff High School, Cardiff

Kaká

Forever running, like a river.
A sturdy rock, that keeps its composure.
He's like Powerade,
Full of energy and has a good kick.

Like a bold, graceful eagle,
He smartly plays his game.
With the precision and perfection
Of an experienced puma.

Like the Canadian Red Oak,
He's at the very top of football.
He is, of course, Kaká.

Elliot Stockford (14)
Cardiff High School, Cardiff

The Fearless Dragons

Withdrawn you tremble down at their feet;
An emerald-ruby pair of eyes.

Such majesty, no one could ever deny,
With passion, spreading their wings to fly.

Great roaring voices travel across the hill and vale,
To be recorded and heard in many tales.

Amber eyes stare down upon the earth;
Filled with power, like fires from the herd.

I see them as the spirit of creature,
From valley, to the open space.

Each one locked within our very heart,
Waiting to be unleashed, to be free from, but never apart.

Megan Evans (12)
Cardiff High School, Cardiff

The Sun

It is a beacon of light
Shining brightly in the sky.

It can be a burning hell above our heads
Or a mother to Earth's striving life.

The burning eye stares at the world
Guarding Man from the darkness of night

Giving life to all who want it
And without it no fish could swim
And no bird would fly.

Kian Maheri (15)
Cardiff High School, Cardiff

Life Story Of A Coin

In the mud I glimpse something shine.
I pick up the coin, worn faceless by time.
I wonder how it came to fall in the gutter.
If it could speak what tales would it utter?

As I hold it gently in my hands,
I wonder has it come from distant lands,
Like Spain perhaps, or distant Morocco,
France, Egypt, Iceland or hot Mexico?

I imagine the joys and sorrows it saw
In times of peace and years of war.
Was it used to buy wedding rings,
Coffins, or toys
As birthday presents for unknown boys?

Dylan Johns (12)
Cardiff High School, Cardiff

The Beast

I have tamed the rhino inside me.
My thick, hard skin keeps it in.

My black eyes are focused
The huge horns are not needed
And refused despite my feet big as ever.

The nostrils I was handed
Breathe out fiery, hot air
And in a flash I'm short-tempered.
And then I could run a marathon.

Don't mess with the beast
For it spells danger.

Tom Hatch (15)
Cardiff High School, Cardiff

The Place I Know

The place I know,
is famous for mining.
It has cities and villages,
and places to dine in!

The place I know,
has sheep galore.
With museums and galleries,
it is never a bore!

The place I know,
has a dragon on its flag.
With the colours red, white and green,
even from afar it looks no rag!

The place I know,
has a brilliant rugby team.
When they play at the Millennium Stadium,
it is a fantastic scene!

The place I know,
has a male voice choir.
Plus Charlotte Church and Tom Jones,
they sing lower and sing higher.

The place I know,
is steeped in history and tales.
It is the place I was born,
can you guess? . . . It is *Wales!*

Jessica Schwartz (12)
Cardiff High School, Cardiff

Wanderer

He wanders
No direction or destination
No aim or goal
On he wanders
Through the lands of sorrow and grief
He is long forgotten
On he wanders
The wind howls
A tree rustles
On he wanders
He feels nothing
No pain or sadness
No regret or remorse
Only the silence of the night
So on he wanders.

Joel Gordon (12)
Cardiff High School, Cardiff

Recipe For Wales

Take a handful of rain fallen on Mount Snowden
Mix with a bowlful of Welsh cake batter
Stir until smooth
Add two fluffy white clouds
Leave to rise for eighty minutes and play a game of rugby
Add the petals of a first spring daffodil
And dust from a crumbling castle
Leave to cook while you climb up a mountain
When you return and eat a slice, you will have tasted Wales.

Elin Barrett (13)
Cardiff High School, Cardiff

Wales

Mountain tops sprinkled with snow
The valleys peaceful and quiet
Further down the road
I come to a city
Its hip-hop beat never resting

The sand is a golden dust
With the sea feasting on it greedily
On the other side of the dune I find a port
A busy smoky place
People running everywhere

The old brick castle surrounded by a moat of cars
Inside tourists swarm
I try to imagine it hundreds of years ago
Outside the walls of the castle I find towers of shops
All brightly coloured with fancy displays
Showing off like top models

I arrive at the Millennium Stadium
The whole country seems to have turned up
Excitement buzzes in the air
There are daffodils, flags and plastic leeks being waved
Spirit is everywhere
Unique accents come together as one
When they belt out the Welsh anthem with pride
That's my country
Wales!

Georgina Davies (12)
Cardiff High School, Cardiff

Mystery Of The Deep

Lurking in the murky waters,
Occasionally shifting its indescribable size,
A shadow with no body,
Mystery of the deep.

Silky-smooth oily skin,
Barnacle-covered underbelly,
Misty eyes capable of penetrating the darkest blue,
Mystery of the deep.

Lonely echoing call,
Irregular beat of a flipper,
Silently gliding through the eerie gloom,
Mystery of the deep.

With one swift movement the body heaves and breaks
The frothy surface,
A pause as it hovers in the sea air for a brief moment,
A torrent of water, ten feet high, joins the ocean sounds,
A glass-shattering smack as the tail collides
With the light-touched water,
Plunging back down to the icy depths,
Withdrawing once more to the familiar rocky background,
Mystery of the deep.

Harriet Averill (13)
Cardiff High School, Cardiff

The Storm

The voice of the North Sea moves closer and closer
Frozen lakes of the east call for masters
Wind moves around, lifting you higher and higher into the clouds
The cliffs form a welcoming shelter
The sunrays dance around and they slowly get pushed away by
                                              the weeping goddess

The west wind blows and howls as it fights the beasts of the
                                                            deep sea
Ships rock back and forth and twist and turn
Racing white horses run faster and faster trying to escape from
                                            the depths of the storm
The echoes of the caves ring, calling for help
The shallow darkness starts to swallow up its surroundings

The sea angers, pulling the ships into its grasp
The goddess moans crying for her loved ones
Darkness crawls across the sky
Claws thrust out of darkness clutching at anything in its reach
Bright yellow streaks fall from the sky as the goddess lets go
                                                       of her hair
The sand wraps a thick blanket around the ships as they settle
                                                  on the seabed
The mysterious claws dispatch from the ocean
Valleys of the south pull the goddess towards them
As she rents the air with her screams
The breath of the ocean calms and softly slides away
Leaving just the memories of what had been.

Bryony Anderson (13)
Cardiff High School, Cardiff

Eisteddfed Poem

As the sun slowly rises into the rubescent sky,
Rays of brilliant light creep through the gaps of the proud mountains,
A sweet smell of fresh-baked Welshcake,
Floats along the moist refreshing air,
Daffodils sway in the invigorating breeze,
Dancing like elegant ice skaters on performance night.
A young couple lie by the rocks on a picturesque beach,
As the untamable sea thuds against the rocks.
Newborn lambs' cheerful cries echo,
As they skip around the luscious green field.
Courageous castles stand tall, their walls flooding
With memorable stories and words,
These are never spoken, but you can feel them run through
                                              your body.

This is a wondrous land.
Old and new stories yet to be told.
This is my home.
This is my *Wales*.

Katherine Thomas (14)
Cardiff High School, Cardiff

Football Report

The ball swerved past the post.
The keeper scrambled towards the ball and pushed it away with his glove.
The defender smashed the ball away with his boot.
The adrenalin spurted amidst the anger of the decision.
The excitement increased from the roar of the crowd,
As the ball skimmed the pitch, it destroyed the grass.

The injured player screamed before he even hit the grass.
The striker's head smashed against the post.
A murmur ran throughout the crowd.
The player's face started to bleed as Lehmann punched him with
                                              his glove.
The team had lost the cup because of the poor decision.
The defender aggressively charged towards the ball with his raised boot.

Joshua Moore (15)
Cardiff High School, Cardiff

The Pianist

Once more he stepped into the
Gloom. His polished face was
Gaunt and grey. A wasted man.
A forgotten story put away,
Hidden, joked about, but not
Too much. In Krakow town, he
Sung through bombs and blood
And filthy Berlin angry dogs till
Finally, he got knocked down.

The sailing songs, and tidings strong,
Made women laugh, and men
Shed tears, blush, smoke on,
And mourn through choking
Smog. And in their smoky bars
A distant story could be felt;
A lamp of shadow, deep and hopeful,
A song that never yields, a Krakow
Legend writhing in the dark
Made Krakow hearts stand still and melt.

The keys bounce on like stones
On glass; fade, pale, hounded
By age, tainted by fear
And blood and love.
'Lost forever,' he said, looking
Up. Sad black eyes, snout alert,
Peering at me through grime
And dirt; a ghost, a Jew, a
Prince of thieves. He doesn't hear,
I ask again; he smiles like
All good Polish men.
'What's that you say?' He points
Above: they're tears of winter,
Tears of love.

Daniel Bright (17)
Cardiff High School, Cardiff

Hollywood

We will go to the bright lights,
where even the mud sparkles
like a star in the night sky.
Every paving stone holds
a hint of fame and the glimmers
of hope entwine the people
like stalks of ivy.
The buildings stand as tall
as trees in the rainforest
and as stern as a head teacher.
The shops are expensive
as a shed full of the purest diamonds,
and even the people deserve
purple gowns to leave
their glamorous homes
which hold the key to many secrets.
Stars awaiting their fate
like a baby waiting for its milk,
but what is seen beyond
the bright lights
is not as pretty as a rose
but sometimes as dark as night,

the outside world is exploding.

Sarah Lovell (17)
Cardiff High School, Cardiff

The Newsman

The news at six . . .
Fighting around the world
Reported on a show
A TV belongs to a family
Who gather for the shock.
It's that time again
It's the newsman
Like a robot telling horrific stories,
Sitting reading devastation
And *human* pain.
We are eating our tea
Not knowing the pain that has been caused.
Then four hours later, introduced by a song
He says,
'Hello, this is the News at Ten.' *Bong!*

Michael Dunn (15)
Cardiff High School, Cardiff

Recipe For Wales

Take the patriotism of St David,
Mix with the hospitality of the native Welsh people,
Marinate in Cymraeg.

Chop up the freshly baked Welsh cakes,
Stir in a generous helping of lush green pastures,
Leave to set in a few sun-kissed daffodils.

Fold in the serenity of Dylan Thomas' literature,
Whisk in a handful of peace,
Add a dash of Princess Diana's aura.

Stir in some spiralling roads from Heaven,
Flame grill with a Welsh dragon's fierce fire,
Garnish with true Welsh wool.

Maha Naeem (13)
Cardiff High School, Cardiff

The Reverse

Numb, as I prepared to be forever scarred,
Helpless, as the doctors refused to look at me,
Horror-struck, as I first looked at my reflection in the glass window,
Confused, when I saw my mother screaming in shock,
Blank, as I lifted my head,
Weeping, as my friends and comrades fell,
Shaking, as the shells flew ahead,
Nervous, as the day was announced,
Anxious, when I first lay down in my trench,
Fearless, as I flew to the Somme,
Awe-struck, by my first experience of the weapons,
Excited, as I left for the training camp,
Confident, as I signed the army application form.

Yousaf Jamal
Cardiff High School, Cardiff

A Unique Place

Crispy grass,
A fresh blanket of white snow on top,
Clear water droplets seeping off the tree leaves,
Icy cold slush oozing off an abandoned bridge,
Frosty blue opals scattered across a path,
On top of a sheet of ice,
The sun peeking out of the clouds,
Gleaming on a frozen pond,
A flicker of light,
A shimmery shine,
A woodpecker situated on a branch,
Creating a distinct mark in the bark,
Elegant orchids swaying in the wintry breeze,
Dry leaves drifting; into a unique place.

Tabitha Kearney (12)
Cardiff High School, Cardiff

The Story Of The Burning Planet

We live in a world which is slowly slipping from our grasp,
Stained and exhausted by the industrial class,
There's a law to be brainwashed before we can pass
Through life.

We live in a world being swallowed by its own creation,
Distressingly destroyed by Man's dictation,
It will never be handed its liberation
From death.

> *What has become of our society*
> *Where crooks are given the authority?*
> *A world run by villains is not for me,*
> *So I'll remain with the minority.*

We live in a world which we could save if we wanted to,
Call for a rescue and see it through,
There's always something we can do,
To pull our world back.

> *What has become of our society*
> *Where crooks are given the authority?*
> *A world run by villains is not for me,*
> *So I'll remain with the minority.*

Luke James (17)
Cardiff High School, Cardiff

Land Of Our Fathers

The glittering jewel in the crown,
A million poets could not describe,
Majesty of the open plains,
Splendour of the mountain peaks,
A snow-topped peak above the world.

The fury of an everlasting darkness,
Engulfing the highest land,
Waves of impossible fury,
Crashing down upon the sands,
Destroying the defences.
Castles to the north,
Castles to the south,
Courage is great behind the castle's walls,
On the open fields,
Heroes will arise!

Peter Lloyd-Williams (12)
Cardiff High School, Cardiff

It . . .

In my world,
It lurks,
So full of hatred,
From its lonely years,

Bombs,
Unexploded bombs,
Its territory,
No-man's-land,

Blood,
Just dripping metallic blood,
Is all that remains,
From its lonely years,

So saddened,
From its lonely years.

It . . .

James Grace (14)
Cardiff High School, Cardiff

The Life Of A Bully

I am the boy that walks down the street.
The boy that people like to pick on.
I just want to live my life,
But at the moment, nothing's going right.

In school, the bullies always come up to me,
Their faces always filled with glee.
They push and shove me to the ground,
But there's nothing I can do, they always get me down.

I want to fight back but I'm too scared,
What shall I do? There's no help, or is there?
Or am I just not helping myself?

Jake Rooney (13)
Denbigh High School, Denbigh

Through The Eyes Of A Little Boy In Iraq

Every day we live in fear,
I see my mother shed a tear.
We've got the army at our door,
Dead and injured, there are more and more.
In Iraq we used to have pride,
Now we live in fear and hide.
To see our family members die,
It's just so hard not to cry.
Americans and Britons everywhere.
It makes our country look so bare.
Mr Bush, but what for.
Making this unwanted war.
When will it stop?
Or is it just the start?
You're tearing Iraq apart!

Stephanie Farley (13)
Denbigh High School, Denbigh

Homeless Person

I am on the streets,
All alone and scared,
Everyone walks past and always stares.

My belly is rumbling,
Every minute of the day,
I don't know why,
But I know I need some food today.

I may have to rummage in the rubbish bin,
Sometimes it can be a sin,
I might find a half-eaten butty,
But it's better than a rotten shoe.

This is my life,
This is how I live.

Lisa Davies (13)
Denbigh High School, Denbigh

Untitled

All of the people are scared of him,
You mess with him, you'll be in the bin,
He walks around with his crew,
The leader goes by the name of Andrew.

They hang around by the park,
They stay out late in the dark,
They take no rubbish from anyone,
If someone comes, they'll soon be gone.

They go around robbing the shop,
The police chase them and shout, 'Stop!'
They share the money between them all,
But the leader always gets some more.

They go around beating people up,
Most of them just get back up,
I wait for the day that someone will say,
'Do that again and I'll hit you one day!'

One day they get caught,
I feel better now justice is bought,
They are banged away for a long time,
Now we can all have a happy time.

Ben Lovell (13)
Denbigh High School, Denbigh

Stupid Dictionary

I am a stupid dictionary, old and bored
Last bit of fun was when that kid shouted and roared
I have been spat on
I have been sat on
I'm a stupid dictionary, old and bored
I'm always being thrown at the board!

I'm a stupid dictionary, old and sad
Last time I was happy was when the little kids went mad
I have been ripped
I have been kicked
I'm a stupid dictionary, old and sad
This class is boring and bad

I'm a happy dictionary, new and clever
I'm always being used by all of Class Seven
People read me
People succeed with me
I'm a happy dictionary new and better
So much better than the stupid old dictionary.

Liam Rowlands (14)
Denbigh High School, Denbigh

Why?

Just when I thought my life couldn't get much worse,
We found out my father had AIDS,
He had been ill for quite a while,
I had a rough idea what was wrong with him,
Because AIDS is such a common thing round here.
It's what my mother died from,
So I know the signs of it.
I feel terrible because there's not a lot more I can do
To help my dad get better.
It's horrible seeing him lying there in the condition he's in,
Really it is.

I am the eldest out of us six children,
My brothers and sisters, are aged between three and eleven,
If my father goes to Heaven, I will be responsible for them all,
I already do my best at looking after them,
As well as collecting water from a well about 3½ half miles away,
Cleaning our hut,
Making sure there's enough food, which there hardly ever is,
It really is hard going for us and all I can do is live each day
                                                         as it comes,

But there's one thing I don't understand . . .
Why is it happening to me? Why me?
Why are we the ones with such a poor country?

Chelsea Wynne (14)
Denbigh High School, Denbigh

Through The Eyes Of A Disability

Why do people stop and stare?
Why should they care?
People always look me up and down,
As if I were a clown.

Why do I feel so insecure,
When people come knocking at my door?
I'm worried about the way I look,
I'm sure they think of me as a crook!

Why am I an outcast?
I don't even fit in with my class!
Sometimes I need a helping hand,
To get me on my feet and mend.

I wish I were a normal girl,
Who lived in an ordinary world.
I won't live till I'm old,
People are always cold.

I would love to be free,
Search the world, climb a tree,
I would love to be like every other child,
I would love to swim a mile.

I want people to stop and care,
Not stop and stare!
I want the world to change,
I want people to know my name.

Ceri Jones (13)
Denbigh High School, Denbigh

'So-Called Friends': Through The Eyes Of . . .

It's Saturday morning once again,
I'm off to see my so-called friends,
They said, 'Meet us at the ancient train.'
But where are they? I knew they'd pretend.

I'm waiting on the edge,
Trains are flying by,
I hear footsteps from behind the hedge,
I'm going to cry.

It's them, they grab me,
Chuck me onto the tracks,
I scream, there's a train coming straight for me . . .
Smack!

Ella Richards (13)
Denbigh High School, Denbigh

Through The Eyes Of . . .

I am woken up by guns
I can hear the screams of fallen men
My heart is full of sorrow
I fear there's no tomorrow.

I see one of my men
Shot down lying there
All his body is showered with blood
With his face's empty stare.

I've climbed out of my truck now
Into no-man's-land
Bombs are falling hard now
Death is all around now.

Robert Jones (13)
Denbigh High School, Denbigh

Through The Eyes Of Guy

I'm that guy that nobody likes,
I'm that guy that wants to cry,
I just want to run away
And see a smile again someday.

I'm that guy that nobody likes,
I'm that guy that wants to cry,
I just want to live my life,
Live the life nobody likes.

I'm that guy that nobody likes,
I'm that guy that wants to cry,
In a cave . . . away from sight,
Away from sun that shines so bright.

Yes, I'm that guy that wants to hide,
I'm that guy that's bullied for life,
I'm that guy that's in this state,
I'm that guy that has no mates.

Dion Lloyd-Williams (14)
Denbigh High School, Denbigh

My Great Nan

Her skin is like silk.
She is as kind as a nurse.
She is as old as the Stone Age.
Her hair is always curly like a pig's tail.
Her hair is as grey as a cloud.
I love my nan!

Sarah Rees (11)
Dyffryn Comprehensive School, Port Talbot

What Is Red?
(Based on 'What is Pink?' by Christina Rossetti)

What is red?
Blood is red
From people that are dead

What is blue?
The sky is blue
Like a smooth blue glue

What is yellow?
The sun is yellow
And is always mellow

What is black?
Space is black
Always staring back

What is grey?
A shark is grey
Hope you're not its prey

What is white?
Clouds are white
Always fluffy and light

What is green?
Grass is green
With bugs in-between

What is pink?
A princess is pink
Who has a boat that sinks

What is brown?
Mud is brown
Which makes mothers frown

What is gold?
A crown is gold
But is very cold

What is orange?
An orange is orange
Just an orange, a plain orange.

Jacob Davies (12)
Dyffryn Comprehensive School, Port Talbot

The Soul Piper

The soul piper, piping his way like a sniper.
Playing with children who don't know they're dead.
And when realised, are sent to Heaven's bed.
But those who revenge go back to where they died
And are dragged to Hell when the piper's one-eyed.
The spell will arise, thunder, lightning,
Water, water everywhere but not a drop to drink.
This is the music which will make you think.
Carry me always, carry me well
For this is the creature of herb and spell.
It is the link to power arcane
Forget it and thy magic shall wane.
Curses, curses, alchemy
Everything will be scary,
These secrets shall be thine, through he.
But readers remember above all this;
This creature is not that in mud that crawls.
And forever doomed shall be the one
Who betrays his secrets one by one.

Lois Samuel (11)
Dyffryn Comprehensive School, Port Talbot

The Robin

As I awoke one morning
The air was soft and still
And then I saw a robin
Perched on my window sill
Slowly I pulled back the bedclothes
And tiptoed out of bed
But when I got to the window
The robin had already fled!

Charli Davies (12)
Dyffryn Comprehensive School, Port Talbot

Outlands

As I walk through this forsaken land
Where trees barely grow
And light barely shines
I think, *how did this happen?*

The scars of war,
The wounds of pollution,
Infect this land
With the poison of corruption
I think, *how did this happen?*

A dreaded ruler,
Of a sickening race
Mutated and agonistic
As they lie, screaming.

But maybe there is hope,
We could save this place, this outland,
If we keep on fighting this plague
Until death do us part.

Jamie Hewitt (14)
Elfed High School, Buckley

Summer

The sky is clear blue, not a cloud in sight.
The soft golden sand lies on the ground.
The cool light breeze brushes silently against their backs
As the red-hot sun blazes down onto them.

Their five smiles shine like white pearls,
Their golden hair reflects the sunlight,
Their beautiful big blue eyes look out across the sea,
What a perfect day in the summer it will be.

Rhian Taylor (14)
Elfed High School, Buckley

Fashion

Who's wearing what?
Who's worn it where?
Some people scoff,
That they just don't care.

I have to disagree,
This is just not true!
People change their clothes,
Till they're positively blue.

Hats, scarves, bags and shoes,
Colours, materials, accessories are there.
Gucci, Chanel, Dior and Ghost,
You've got the list,
Now what should you wear?

Prada bags, Beyonce's got two,
Mariah's got seven.
For a normal person like me,
To own just one,
Would be absolute heaven!

Kate Openshaw (15)
Elfed High School, Buckley

Stereotypes

Remarks shouted wherever you go,
people can't just leave you alone,
pushed, shoved, mocked and picked on,
why can't you be your character's reflection?

Why is it so important to others,
that you are not like the latter?
Does personality not matter?

Why is it that people are so shallow?
One person changes and others follow,
why does it matter what you wear,
when it should only be you who cares?

Katy Healing (15)
Elfed High School, Buckley

Ruined!

Something's changed in all my friends,
They no longer talk, of when it ends,
The sorrow follows over every man,
They don't even think of fame and glam,
The glory ideas that brightly shone,
Now, unwillingly, they have gone.

These bodies move but their spirits have died,
As they feed bullets to the other side,
We know the men we fight and kill,
All are weak and many ill,
But we can't stop,
It's not our choice,
And on and on our conscience's voice,
We have no hope, we'll see no end,
In our trenches years we spend.

I'm not a coward, of that I'm sure,
But I can't take this anymore,
My friends' voices go through my head,
But why does it matter because they're dead?

I'm all alone,
Just in this field,
I'm eighty-six and move on wheels,
See I have no legs and I have no friends,
So sure enough I will be dead.

So for all you brave young men out there,
Don't go to war, don't you dare,
Because I'm the last,
My life will soon end,
And years in regret I know you will spend.

Ashleigh Boyle (14)
Elfed High School, Buckley

People

It's sad when people you know
Become people you used to know
When you can walk right past someone
As if they were never a big part of your life
How you spent hours together talking
And now you can barely look at them
But what you wouldn't give
To have them back once more
To hear their voice and to see their face again
Not just be a distant memory
Of how things used to be
Before that silly quarrel
Quite some time ago.
Nothing lasts forever, so live life to the full
And take the good things with the bad
As one day everything will be
Exactly as you want it to be
So no tears and no regrets
Look forward to tomorrow
And all that it will bring
You only get one shot at it
So grab it while you can.

Caia Stevenson (15)
Elfed High School, Buckley

Saturday

Early start
Grey skies
Shouting dads
Moaning mums
Tense manager
Eager players
Tiring warm-up
3 o'clock kick-off
Hard challenges
Clever passes
Powerful shots
Spectacular saves
Cheering crowd
Cheating dives
Frustrated coach
Half-time
Welcome drink
Treated injuries
Yelling manager
Motivated players
Obscene gestures
Yellow card
Poor referee
Brazilian skills
Winning goal
Filthy kit
Tired legs
Proud team
Shiny trophy!

Richard Williams (14)
Elfed High School, Buckley

My First Race

As I sit in my car,
looking at the red light
driving my Texas Star
can you feel my fright?

as the light turns green
we're off at 100 miles per hour
hitting it up to 3rd
we're on the first corner

I don't think I can last
number 30 is right behind me
I'm stuck in my seat
1st position I can see

it's a race in itself
I'm in first place
I can see the line
it's once again my race

as I cross the line
1st place I have won
the crowd goes wild
the glistening of the sun
I can see the face of the little kid's smile

This race has brought my glory!

Sean Hughes (15)
Elfed High School, Buckley

Anonymous

My friends, at least I think they're my friends,
Treat me like I'll always be there,
But what happens when one day I'm not?
Would anyone even notice?
Would anyone even care?

Why do they think they can treat me like dirt
When all I've ever wanted from them was to be seen?
Why do the things they say always hurt?
They don't realise what they do to me is mean.

They think they can go on discarding my feelings,
When inside all along I've been reeling,
They don't understand,
How each lay of their hand,
Is becoming less and less appealing.

When will they realise that I am a human being
Not just an object of abuse?
They think I am a tool of unlimited use,
When will they open their eyes and start seeing?

Now, I realise people,
I have in the past called friends
Are no more than insignificant trends.
Although they'll never know it,
They were the big black hole in my life,
And the result of this was,
My final insignificant end.

Luke Webster (14)
Elfed High School, Buckley

The Point Of It All

What's the meaning of life?
Is it to live and learn
Or is it to destroy and burn?
No, be honest, I don't know.

We live one day to another,
Never knowing what's going to happen,
Is life worth the bother?
Ask yourself someday.

We destroy what we create,
People call it human nature,
I call it the urge to desecrate,
For we have a habit of ruining the things we treasure most.

So look upon tomorrow,
For the signs that will change yours and my life,
For some, a day to celebrate, others, a day of sorrow,
Just remember you only live once.

Jake Anglesey (14)
Elfed High School, Buckley

Hidden Tears

I lie alone so still I lie
The silent tears I seem to cry
Burning at my raging heart
Keeping us so far apart

The way you seem to look at me
Is this the way it has to be?
A distant smile you glance at me
Is this the way we chose to be?

Every heartbeat that I feel
Every movement that I make
Reminds me of you
And the things I must do.

Siân Evans (15)
Elfed High School, Buckley

You Don't Know Me

He tries to suppress his gross desires,
He grows old but never tires.
His mind is a maze, built like a tomb,
He and fate decide your doom.

He catches you with that casual glance,
His funny way of asking for a dance.
He takes you home; a one-night stand,
And he caresses with a loving hand.

He kisses your face, he kisses your neck,
You're turned on, a nervous wreck.
And that is when he takes a bite,
Drinks your blood and then takes flight.

They find your body, dry and alone,
Meanwhile, the vampire flies back home.
He climbs into his coffin, unhappy, but full,
He closes the lid, and all is dull.

He hates what he's done,
He tries not to think,
Of that woman's flesh
Where his teeth did sink!

Samantha Shaw (15)
Elfed High School, Buckley

The Countryside

A lot of people often take things for granted,
The people they love and also the flowers that are planted.
The leaves on the trees
And in their hives, the buzzy bees.
There have been huge forests in the past,
But how long will the rest last?
They are being torn apart,
And breaking the big wildlife heart.
The grass is no longer green,
As that beautiful time has already been.

Samantha Hird (15)
Elfed High School, Buckley

Earth

There are so many theories of how I began,
Was there a big bang, or did God make it all?
In times of old, priests thought
Everything revolved around me,
But, oh no, I go round the sun,
Modern day people abuse me,
With their trash and pollution,
But they better watch out,
Money won't buy anything,
When there's nothing left to buy!

Laura Martin (13)
Hawarden High School, Hawarden

Titanic

Sailing joyfully
Then *thump,*
Down, down, she sunk.

A tragic time that took many lives.
On the 10th April 1912, the Titanic took sail.
Largest most luxurious ship in those times.
The ship was filled from head to tail.

Sailing joyfully
Then *thump,*
Down, down, she sunk.

The crew had been warned several times.
She was travelling at the speed of 20.5 knots.
Then three hours later
She began to sink.

Sailing joyfully
Then *thump,*
Down, down, she sunk.

1,500 people died and only 700 survived.
All those precious lives.
From newborn to many old.
Why? Oh why?

Sailing joyfully
Then, thump,
Down, down, she sunk.

She carried some of the richest.
She carried many powerful.
People's fortunes were worth $600 million at that time
Yet a lot were poor.

Sailing joyfully
Then *thump,*
Down, down, she sunk.

Sailing joyfully
Then, *thump,*
Down, down, she sunk.

Leah Edwards (13)
Hawarden High School, Hawarden

Through My Telescope

Nothing but darkness,
They should be coming soon,
There, a glimmer of light,
Yes! The stars and the moon.

I steady my telescope,
Put my eye to the hole,
Then what a surprise,
Look up and behold!

Venus is shimmering,
Mars is shining bright,
The stars are gazing down at me,
The moon giving endless light.

But what else is up there,
With the stars, planets and the moon?
It's so big, there could be anything,
I've got to find out soon.

Then a streak of light,
Moving quite slow,
Could it be a shooting star
Or a UFO?

Does space go on forever?
Are aliens a trick of the eye?
Are we the only humans?
If so, soon our race will die!

So, what else is up there
With the stars, planets and the moon?
It's so big, there could be anything,
I've got to find out soon.

Megan Brooke-Jones (11)
Hawarden High School, Hawarden

From The Heart, The Soul

Since I was a newborn child,
I have had the very best of friends,
She has made me strong,
She has made me proud,
So I never want to let her down,
But she has done her part,
So I'll do mine,
For she is the one who made my life,
So I stand before my peers and vow,
I will pay her back . . .
Someday,
Somehow,
I will buy her a tulip,
I will buy her a rose,
I will search and scour until I know,
What it is like to create a smile,
Or if it is worth that while,
I will be there forever and a day,
For the woman who made me this way . . .

Mum!
I love you xxxx

Eleanor Anne Wyndham Badhams (13)
Hawarden High School, Hawarden

Terror

Imagine,
Imagine having no one to talk to,
Imagine having no care in your life,
Imagine getting beaten every night until you were blue,
Imagine every night hearing screaming, shouting and smashes,
Imagine your parents shouting slurred drunken words at you,
Imagine living in an awful painful silence,
Imagine every little hope you had, broken bit by bit,
Imagine living a life of terror,
Imagine this is you . . .

Polly Mewse (12)
Hawarden High School, Hawarden

Madeleine McCann's Disappearance

Madeleine disappeared on the third of May,
While her parents went out to eat,
Just before her fourth birthday,
Since then, there has been much deceit.
Her parents are trying to be strong,
'We want you back where you belong.'

Her parents came back to the hotel apartment,
But to the shock of them, she wasn't there,
Then they got involved with the Portuguese police department,
Her parents cried, 'It's not fair!'
Her parents are trying to be strong,
'We want you back where you belong.'

Under every country's sky,
Everyone has shown their support in many ways,
Hopes to find her are high,
She has been missing for over two hundred days
Her parents are trying to be strong,
'We want you back where you belong.'

Kathryn Wakley (12)
Hawarden High School, Hawarden

Time To Jump

I look out into this wide-open space
My eyes dart around, looking all over the place
I hear every noise, every tiny sound
There goes the bell and I start my round
I hear the crowd, my muscles tense
As I prepare myself for the very first fence
I feel the grip at the end of the reins
Put my trust in my rider, feel the wind through my mane.
I am up and over and galloping on
I explode over the next one like an atom bomb
I feel the pressure urging me on
Over the finish line and we have won!

Jessica Bennett (12)
Hawarden High School, Hawarden

Aberfan Ballad

This is the story of the Aberfan disaster
It was the biggest tragic event
That their lives had ever spent . . .

The day was the 21st October 1966.
It was on a school day,
When the teachers were going to say,
'Go to your first lesson.'
It was certainly the biggest session!

Poor children,
Poor children.

The time was nine-fifteen to be precise.
First the fog held up the rescuers,
And then suddenly one tripped over a log
Trying to find the school.

Poor children,
Poor children.

A huge coal slag heap came towards the school,
Then buried them all.
The rescuers gave them a call,
But then it was too late.

Poor children,
Poor children.

Inside, it was all crushed and damaged,
They tried and tried but they could not manage.
At least eighty-five children had been confirmed dead,
It left a huge lump of coal and everyone's dread.

Poor children,
Poor children.

They said it was the workmen's fault,
But nobody knew.
It will stay in the minds of families,
All life through,
They said it shouldn't have happened.

Poor children,
Poor children.

It was just around the corner,
Not very far away.
Why couldn't they live for another day?
It was at Aberfan, near Merthyr Tydfil in Wales.

Bethan Snowden-Jones (12)
Hawarden High School, Hawarden

Pollution

I woke up one morning and switched on the news
Pollution
Pollution
Pollution

The air was dirty and the sky was grey,
Rubbish on the ground and underground
Pollution
Pollution
Pollution.

Go down into the countryside,
The air is dirty, the sky is grey,
People coughing, people choking.

Pollution
Pollution
Pollution.

Go down into the hills,
The air is dirty, the sky is grey.

It's our future,
Please don't throw it away!

Sophie-Lynne Williams (13)
Hawarden High School, Hawarden

The Titanic Tragedy

All were excited to be,
On her maiden voyage,
They waved as she set out to sea,
Little did they know tragedy was upon them.

Whilst wealthy sailed in luxury,
Second class was a different thing,
But both ended up with the same story,
A race for their lives, hoping and praying.

Beautiful as she was,
Twenty lifeboats were all she had
Many lives were lost because,
Passengers preferred to think of the good
Rather than the bad.

April 14th was the ill-fated day,
Through frozen snow and ice,
The Titanic made her way,
And because of the ship's route, lives were the price.

Supposedly, the safest ship ever built,
Was now on her way to the sea floor,
All it took was an iceberg,
And then the Titanic was no more.

When men were not allowed to escape,
Many wives decided to stay,
Their names forever immortalised,
And forever we'll remember that tragic day.

Down, down, sink to the ground
Sacrifice, selfishness and despair
Down, down, sink to the ground,
A watery grave, she's still lying there.

Shannon Brooks (13)
Hawarden High School, Hawarden

Aberfan

Nobody would listen to what they said
The children were singing but would soon be dead
Then there was a rumble underground
    Get them out
    Get them out

It sounded like lightning
It must have been very frightening
They stood still not knowing what would happen
    Get them out
    Get them out

They didn't see the mountain slide
It was collapsing before their eyes
It was too late, it was just about to hit
    Get them out
    Get them out

It happened in 1966
But they only found school bricks
People rushed to shovel out the rubble
    Get them out
    Get them out

The mothers were crying
Not knowing if their child was alive or dying
With fathers digging
    Get them out
    Get them out

116 children died that day
What did the parents get, not even a say
And all because the workers didn't listen
    It's too late,
    It's too late!

Joe Turner (12)
Hawarden High School, Hawarden

My Poem On Space

I went to space one day,
To do an investigation,
As I was walking by,
Something popped out and said,
'Hello, we have come from planet Mars,
We are doing an investigation on humans.'

So I said, 'I will help you,
I have come from planet Earth,
To do an investigation on aliens!
Are you aliens?'
They replied, 'Yes, are you a human?'
I said, 'Yes, perhaps we could help each other.'
They replied, 'OK.'

So we helped each other,
And I took a picture of us!
But the aliens went mad!
Because the flash scared them.
They jumped everywhere,
But then a beam came and took them away.

Meanwhile, as I was on my way home,
I saw the same aliens that had appeared before,
They waved and waved until,
They realised it was me!
They got a massive alien
And it attacked my ship!
Later I apologised and they offered me a lift home!

Samantha Lawson (11)
Hawarden High School, Hawarden

Christmas

Cold frosty air and a low setting sun,
Everyone wrapped up for a winter stroll
Faces full of joy, happiness and fun
Listen intently to jingle bell toll
It is that magical time once a year
Mince pies, mistletoe, holly and spiced wine
A family togetherness, and cheer
Logs on the fire, trees smelling of pine
Children's faces glowing, it's time for bed
Presents wrapped and loaded in Santa's sack
Mum kisses goodnight to those sleepyheads
Santa dressed in red suit and boots so black
It is a wonderful time, full of cheer
Merry Christmas and a happy New Year!

Chelsie Davies (12)
Hawarden High School, Hawarden

Winter Wonderland

As all the trees are almost bare,
And the temperature starts to fall,
Little white crystals start to appear.
As the sun goes down and the moon comes out,
I hear a little pitter-patter on my bedroom window.
In the morning as I peer outside,
I see a blanket of white snow covering the ground.
Icicles hanging down from the rooftops,
Little robins snuggled in their feathers to keep warm,
Blackbirds trying to get worms from the frozen ground,
What a wonderful sight to see!

Sarah Stachowski (12)
Hawarden High School, Hawarden

Solar System Soccer

The sun was in goal,
defending with all his might.

Mercury and Venus were standing,
but defending tight.

Earth, Mars and Jupiter in midfield,
look out! The ball's been back-heeled!

On the side was Saturn,
showing the team a tackling pattern.

And there was Neptune,
shooting at goal.

He whacked the ball with all his might,
it hit the back of the net at the speed of

                              a *meteorite!*

Kelly Evans (11)
Hawarden High School, Hawarden

A Comet's Tale

My journey has begun again,
Along a mystic starry lane.
A three-quarter century has passed,
Since the time you saw me last.

Each wondrous planet that I see,
Fills my heart with joy and glee.
I've found my favourite one of all,
The Earth, that little blue-green ball.

So look for me on the darkest night,
Come join me on my lonely flight.
I'll put a smile upon your face,
As we zoom around in outer space!

Caitlin Taylor (11)
Hawarden High School, Hawarden

Mum!

Mum, you're ever so gorgeous and great,
There's nothing about you that I hate,
With a great big smile,
You're always worthwhile,
Mum . . .
You're the best thing in the world . . .

Mum, you're ever so groovy and nice,
You never judge things on the price,
With lovely blue eyes,
You're the perfect size,
Mum . . .
You're the best thing in the world . . .

Mum, you're ever so caring and kind,
There's nothing else on my mind,
With great advice,
You're always precise,
Mum . . .
You're the best thing in the world . . .

Sophie Evans (12)
Hawarden High School, Hawarden

My Dog

My dog is . . .
Ball popper,
Game stopper,
Lively walker,
Barking talker,
Cat chaser,
Sock misplacer,
Postman eater,
Game beater,
Territory marker,
Endless barker,
Collar wearer,
Bird scarer,
Cheesy grinner,
Race winner,
Noise maker,
Food taker,
Footy player,
Annoying delayer,
Snack muncher,
Dog bone cruncher.

He is playful and noisy,
Silence breaker.

Bryony Stark (13)
Hawarden High School, Hawarden

A Mother Is . . .

Clothes washer,
House cleaner,
Music listener,
Personal chauffeur,
Ace gardener,
Chore reminder,
TV watcher,
Homework checker,
Diary reader,
Hair cutter,
Clothes shopper,
Shoe shiner,
Cake baker,
Hug giver,
Tear mopper,
Cold healer,
Food cooker,
Soothing talker,
Hot water bottle filler,
Mother!

Jessie St Clair (13)
Hawarden High School, Hawarden

Titanic Ballad

On April 14-15th, 1912
The Titanic crashed hard
It was so dreadful for a beautiful boat
All new, never used, so bad
So sad
So sad

On that lovely night
At 2.20 it collided so loud
The boat crashed so hard
It crashed into one huge iceberg
So sad
So sad

So many lives were lost
Over 1,500 lives were sold
All lost in the sea
All lying there in the freezing cold
So sad
So sad

So many, so few survived
Only 724 lives were saved
All lonely and nearly dead
So horrible, so bad
So sad
So sad

The Titanic sank so quickly
Side to side the passengers went
It all happened so fast
It was so dreadfully leant
So sad
So sad

The boat split into two
All damaged and beautiful
Never to reach its destiny
Never planned to break, so graceful
So sad
So sad!

Bethany Evans (12)
Hawarden High School, Hawarden

My Christmas

Shall I tell you my ideal Christmas?
When everyone is in the festive mood,
And outside it's cold with frost on the grass,
Baking the cake and preparing the food.
On Christmas Day we open our presents,
Then play with them all, until dinner time,
For dinner we have chicken and pheasants,
And we flavour them with lemon and lime.
At Grandma's we arrive on Boxing Day,
To enjoy a few drinks and lots of food,
We eat lots of food and find games to play,
Grandad tells some jokes which are sometimes rude.
I love Christmas and look forward to it,
Specially the Christmas lights when they are lit.

Sara Perrett (12)
Hawarden High School, Hawarden

Out Of Space!

I looked up into the sky and searched for all of the planets
looking back at me.
I searched for Mercury, Venus and Mars
but all I saw were bright stars.

I looked again and all I saw was something glowing
this glow was glowing back at me,
it was the moon staring back at me.
I found Mercury and Venus but I didn't see Mars,
I saw stars. The stars looked like silk just like the Milky Way.

I couldn't find any other planets today,
but next time I hope to see Saturn, Uranus, Mars, Jupiter,
Neptune, Pluto and Earth looking right down on me.

Lucy Birchall (11)
Hawarden High School, Hawarden

The Fateful Day

A sea of red and white descended upon Hillsborough on that
                                                          April afternoon
The 1986 FA Cup semi-final would have been decided soon
Liverpool and Forest were warming up on the pitch
Lots of fans were still outside, there seemed to be a hitch.

The Liverpool fans sang, 'You'll never walk alone'
Thousands of Scousers in their recognisable tone
Red scarves aloft above their heads
Not knowing this would be a fateful day for the Reds

At the Leppings Lane end, the turnstiles were struggling to cope
Would they get in the ground on time? The fans were full of hope
Five thousand fans still outside and the match had started
To get the fans in to see the game, the gates were parted

Eight minutes gone and the fans surged forward towards the fence
Spilling onto the pitch, none of it seemed to make sense
The authorities thought this pitch invasion was the work of hooligans
Not realising that help was needed for the fans

The terraces were so full, the fans surged forward with a rush
The crash barriers gave way and there was a horrific crush
The scene was total mayhem, people everywhere in a ruck
Ninety-six fans died that day, when this disaster struck

On Merseyside, in the following days, grief was outpoured
Questions were asked and the Sun newspaper outlawed
People queued outside Anfield to lay flowers on the 'Cop'
The enquiry declared all-seater stadiums, would future disasters stop.

Daniel Williams (13)
Hawarden High School, Hawarden

Love Effects

The fire of love is blazing in my heart
Stormy days windy days, perfect days
Together, forever, we will not part
The burning eyes of thee are in my gaze.

Hearts are pounding as our love-filled eyes meet
Your embrace is forever mine because of our love
My smile gets bigger as we greet
Love is in the air like a flying dove.

Eternal love for each other will not fade
Together, forever, till death we part
Wonders, magic, tremendous things have been made
Meant to be, supposed to be, it's written on my heart.

When I first saw you I flew
With my very last breath I will say, 'I love you!'

Polly Greaves (12)
Hawarden High School, Hawarden

Friends

The friends that you choose are always around,
Showing you that they care for you so much,
When you've fallen out, they'll bring you back round,
And with them you will never lose touch.

Helping you out when you are in trouble,
Nobody can take them away from you,
And to you they are guardian angels,
And forever you will be true to them.

You can tell them your secrets and problems,
Your friends can also give you good advice,
And in their hearts, there you will be welcome,
And to you and others they will be nice.

Friends will always be there to help you out,
Though you argue a lot but do not shout.

Amy Bingham (12)
Hawarden High School, Hawarden

A Brother Is . . .

Nose picker
Lolly nicker
Tongue puller
Morning waker
Hot hugger
Smelly snitcher
Information provider
Sweet asker
Mess maker
Mobile messer
Cake eater
Loud sleeper
Dog kicker
Diary nicker
Fishy feeder
Greedy grudger
Head jumper
Cover nicker
Girly power
Make-up messer
But he is a *star* brother!

Danielle Kaye (12)
Hawarden High School, Hawarden

A (Good) Car Is . . .

Smooth cruising,
Head-turning,
Gas guzzling,
Environmentalist troubling,
Bodywork gleaming,
Race track weaving,
Wheels spinning,
Race winning,
Exhausts flaring,
Tyres wearing,
Brakes screeching,
Extreme speed reaching,
Engine thrashing,
Almost crashing,
Headlights glaring,
To drive this you must be daring!

Liam Ross (13)
Hawarden High School, Hawarden

Exams

Exams are coming
I feel like running
Pressure is rising
Feel like crying
Teachers screaming
Parents beaming
Expectations
Demonstrations
Mock tests and
'Do your best'
Working late and
Tempting fate
Dates are clearer
Coming nearer
Revising French
On the bench
It's getting late
What's my fate?
I've got to go home
I feel all alone
Exams are coming
I feel like running
Pressure is rising
I feel like crying.

Chloe Mancini (14)
Ysgol Bryn Elian, Old Colwyn

Iraq War!

Is it over?
Why is it happening?
Is there much point?
Why can't we stop?

People dying,
People running,
People fighting
And people suffering.

Nuclear weapons
Or just pure stupidity?
Who really knows?
Because I don't.

It's happening,
It's real,
But is there much point?
The answer is *no!*

Samuel Walker (12)
Ysgol Bryn Elian, Old Colwyn

Fashion

Glamorous models
Girly shops
Full of fashion
Shop till you drop!

High street sales
Good stuff there
Lots of bargains
For me to wear.

Make-up, handbags
Shoes and bling
Might treat myself
To a diamond ring!

Geena Watson (13)
Ysgol Bryn Elian, Old Colwyn

Cruelty

Locked up in the shed
The cold floor as my bed,
They pull my ears,
They have done this for years,

Ever since they got their daughter,
I've been put through pain and torture,
They don't care about me, their dog,
They treat me like a rotting log,

I need love and I need care,
Those people burnt off all my hair,
I need help,
They make me yelp! . . .

The RSPCA,
Came next day,
I got put in a big white van,
And my owners got a ban!

I went in a cage for one night only,
And I didn't feel so lonely,
I was locked in a shed,
Now I have a cosy bed.

These people came to meet me,
They will never beat me,
I had a ride in their car,
They took me very far.

I have love and I have care,
These people don't burn my hair!

Charlotte Stephenson (12)
Ysgol Bryn Elian, Old Colwyn

Young Smoking

Stress
People at the age of twelve smoke.
They think it's cool
But they look a fool.

Being cool
Between the ages of ten to sixteen
They think it's cool to smoke
But then it comes to seeing the doctor
That's a big *uh-oh!*

Peer pressure
People say no
But then go and think it's a sweet
The sweet in the shape of a bow!

Stress.
Stress is a big thing
But don't take it out on smoking.
If you think it helps you, it's just a lie
Because then you get addicted and die.

Friends
If you want friends
Don't go and pretend
That you smoke
It's bad for your heart
And lungs.

Hollie Higgins (13)
Ysgol Bryn Elian, Old Colwyn

Stereotypes

All around, there are stereotypes,
That have to look a certain way,
Let's all be individuals,
And let's start from today.

'Never judge a book by its cover',
That's what they say,
But what's happened to that?
It's gone far, far away.

Hair colour, eye colour,
Size and weight,
There is always one thing,
That people will hate.

Goths, emos, chavs,
The list will never end,
Being your own person,
Should be the growing trend.

Tall, skinny,
Short or fat,
You are who you are
And that is that.

You hear people talking,
Saying you are strange,
But maybe it's them,
That really need to change.

All around, there are stereotypes,
That have to look a certain way,
Let's all be individuals,
And let's start from today!

Anna Wilson (14)
Ysgol Bryn Elian, Old Colwyn

Still Human!

The way we're dressed.
The music we listen to.
The people we hang around with.
It's up to us, so why are we judged on it?

Goth,
black hair,
black make-up,
black clothes,
but they're still human!

Chav,
gold rings,
tracksuits,
Burberry,
but they're still human!

Skater,
long hair,
baggy clothes,
skateboard,
but they're still human!

In the end we're all the same,
so we shouldn't be judged by anyone.
The only stereotype we should be under is . . .
Human!

Mathew Roberts (14)
Ysgol Bryn Elian, Old Colwyn

Categories

Plastics, goths and chavs, they are some categories
Plastics known as girls with bleached blonde hair
Handbags by Dior and Chanel
Who's to say they don't think the same?

Separating overweight people from size 0s
Eating disorders in both minds to lose some weight
Under pressure from clothing ranges and models
Who's to say they can't do the same job?

Chavs on street corners, smoking and drinking
Looking for trouble and a prison sentence
Others just dress like chavs in trackies and trainers
Who's to say they are exactly the same?

Tall and short, different sizes, who cares?
They may look different from everyone else
What's wrong with being unique?
Who's to say they can't do the same job?

Goths dressed in black as if they are mourning,
Staying awake till day is dawning
They may look different and weird from everyone else
Who's to say they aren't the same?

Many people do it, maybe even you,
But before you speak, think
Before you act, think
Separating one from another is hurtful,
Remember who's to say we don't feel the same?

Ashleigh Steinson (14)
Ysgol Bryn Elian, Old Colwyn

Lost

Along a row of empty faces,
Hearts are healing empty spaces,
Lives are torn and people cold,
Problems shared and some untold,
People deal in separate ways,
Feeling lonely, losing days,
Everyone's different, life's a song,
With friends your life cannot go wrong,
Sometimes the song is not your track,
You see your story falling back,
People miss you, hearts will break,
Life's a life and yours to take,
If you could see the hurt and pain,
The world's a hard and painful game,
Mountains cry and oceans weep,
Now you're gone, the world will sleep,
Forever you'll live deep in my heart,
Forever together but a lifetime apart.

Jessica Simonds (14)
Ysgol Bryn Elian, Old Colwyn

Drink, Drugs, Rumours And Thugs

Drink, drugs, rumours and thugs,
People bully you for being too weak.
So you sit in a corner and weep.

Drink, drugs, rumours and thugs,
They point and stare because of what you wear.
Because you're a goth, an emo or a chav.

Drink, drugs, rumours and thugs,
They roam the halls thinking they own these walls,
While teachers just stop and stare.

Drink, drugs, rumours and thugs,
Nobody's perfect, nobody's right,
Everyone's looking for a fight.

Max Smith (14)
Ysgol Bryn Elian, Old Colwyn

I Am I

We are trapped in cages so confining,
We can barely breathe.
Our hearts are locked, our wills are tied,
In chains we cannot leave.

These labels are like ropes
Knotted round our minds.
Dividing one from another
Making others blind.

Yet I am I and you are you,
The same and yet apart.
In groups that should not interlace,
Aren't we the same at heart?

So break the shackles that bind you
And step out from your jail.
Embrace the world for what it is
Let all the confines fail.

Don't be afraid to speak your mind,
Free of check or shame.
Stand alone and face the world
Without an ill-acquired name.

Don't be afraid to live and breathe
Or miss the treaded line.
Above all, as you go through life,
Don't be afraid to shine!

Katy Williams (13)
Ysgol Bryn Elian, Old Colwyn

Discrimination

Black, white, orange or pale
does it really matter?
We are who we are, we look how we do,
does it really matter what country we're from?
And should we be punished for people being martyrs,
with war and pain?
Discrimination.

Buddhism, Christianity, Islam or Sikh,
are they really that different?
They all believe there's something, some higher being,
Taoism and Shinto just because they're not well known,
are they any less important?
Discrimination.

Discrimination can lead to war,
but why fight someone who is the same as us
or are we just fighting ourselves?

The world is damaged by our foolishness,
would the world work without humans? Yes!
Would creatures miss us? No!
Are we really that important?
My answer . . . well no!

Laura Rickard (14)
Ysgol Bryn Elian, Old Colwyn

Left Foot Goal

Top trickster
Powerful kickster
Clever midfielder
Defensive shielder
Chance creator
Cocky celebrator
Accurate aim
Puts opponents to shame
Left foot soarer
Straight to the top corner
Never violent
Sneaky and silent
Long ball launcher
Cheeky taunter
Glides down the field with the ball at his feet
Takes the crowd out of their seats
Sneaky ball through
Never gets substitute
Takes the ball through the legs
As the crowd shouts *'Megs!'*
Always the hero
Never a zero!

Josh Monaghan (14)
Ysgol Bryn Elian, Old Colwyn

Stereotypes

Look at that chav over there
Expensive clothes
And spiky hair
Dealing drugs
With his thugs
At the end of the day
It's his choice

Look at that goth over there
Jet-black hair
Don't stop and stare
Just cos he looks a freak
It doesn't mean he is weak
At the end of the day
It's his choice

Look at that skater over there
Baggy jeans
And wacky hair
At the end of the day
It's his choice.

These are all stereotypes
But it's their choice!

Lewis Roberts (13)
Ysgol Bryn Elian, Old Colwyn

Why Be The Same?

Maybe you're different and don't fit in
Being yourself is not a sin.
To be accepted for who you are,
Wherever you're from, near or far.

Being light and skinny or looking good,
Always being laughed at when you fall in the mud.
You should be proud of who you really are,
Confident and happy, shine like a star.

You make that decision as to who you want to become,
Nerves like steel, or is your heart beating like a drum?
Don't be scared of being different inside,
I know it's hard, but you don't have to hide.

Making difficult choices, deciding your fate,
Time is flying so quickly, now is no time to wait.
Enjoy your life and fulfil your dreams,
Although when you're stuck, it's only harder than it seems.

You will do it, fight your way through,
Even if you're lonely and don't know what to do.
Help is always there, somewhere, you'll see,
But only you can decide who you want to be.

Katie Gough (13)
Ysgol Bryn Elian, Old Colwyn

To Be Unique

Why do some people really not care?
Judging you on how you look or the clothes that you wear.
Short, tall, skinny or fat,
None of that matters - remember that!
Blonde hair, brown hair, red or black,
You are who you are and that's a fact!

People judging you and calling you names,
They don't care, to them it's just fun and games.
Black or white, English or Asian,
Why all the hate?
What would it be like if it never had begun?

Goths, chavs, emos and more,
Leave them alone, it's just one big bore!
They are who they are in their own way,
So let them do their own thing and go their own way.

If you're ever feeling down and wondering why,
Ignore all the bullies, just pass them by.
You will always be you, no matter what,
Just stay who you are and like what you've got!

Abbie Wilson (13)
Ysgol Bryn Elian, Old Colwyn

First Impressions

I understand more than you ever will
And less than you could ever imagine
I will never be as beautiful as you
You see, they don't think the inside matters
No matter what they say
I am the nobody that I always was
That little ghost girl
And nothing that anyone can say will change that
Because I have built my life on a web of lies
And they have been perceived as the truth
No one will know who I really am
Wherever I go
I am pretending to be something I'm not
It sickens me, this false charade
But I don't give it up
Because I know that if I do
The reality will come crashing down like thunder
And reality
Will be more
Than I can bear.

Katherine Barnes (14)
Ysgol Bryn Elian, Old Colwyn

Stereotyping

Goths, chavs and plastics,
We are all the same really,
No matter what we look like,
We are all human beings.

Plastics are known for their inch-thick make-up
And long fake hair,
Short skirts and low-cut tops,
Designer handbags and cigarettes.
    This is stereotyping.

Chavs are known for their drinking habits
and tracksuit bottoms,
Smoking fags and fighting,
Gold rings and trainers.
    This is stereotyping.

Goths are known for their black clothing and pale skin,
They may look different to everyone else
But we are all the same underneath.

Natalie Hughes (14)
Ysgol Bryn Elian, Old Colwyn

Daddy's Girl

As I lie tucked up in bed,
I can hear Mummy crying.
Daddy hit her on the head,
I can hear the angels sighing.

Next morning Mummy has a bruise,
I can see that Mummy's crying.
Nana's gone to see the doctor,
I can tell that Nana's dying.

Next day, and I'm going to the zoo,
Daddy's not there, my face falls,
Nana's gone, I miss her too.
I wish Daddy would sometimes call.

Wake up, Mr Policeman's here,
He's pinned Daddy on the floor,
He smiles at me and it is clear,
I can't see Daddy anymore.

It's been two years now and Mummy's dead,
I replay the memories over again.
Sue turns the video off, it's the end,
That's all that's left of Mummy Lorraine.

As I lie tucked up in bed,
I can hear Aunt Susie sighing.
Mummy's gone and Daddy too,
Now I am the one that's crying.

Charlotte Burgess (13)
Ysgol Bryn Elian, Old Colwyn

Teachers

Teachers, teachers, are not nice,
Their hearts are as cold as ice.
They give you homework for something to do,
Even though it's a load of poo.

They force you to get your PE kit,
And play hockey but you get hit.
Being in goal is so mean,
Even though people are keen.

Maths, maths times and division,
The teacher tells you to do revision.

French, French is so bad,
Even though the teacher is mad.

Music, music, is so loud,
And there is a really big crowd.

History, history, is so brill,
And we all sit very still.

Break, break, eat your food
And it puts you in a good mood.

School, school is so pants,
I hope you take notice of my rants!

Conner Bellwood (12)
Ysgol Bryn Elian, Old Colwyn

Friends For Life

F riends, they're just like flowers.
R emember friends are friends.
I can be a good friend
E ven though we might fight, we're still friends.
N ever fancy your boyfriend.
D on't ignore your mates, they
S tick up for you.

F riends are caring.
O nly good people deserve good mates.
R emember a special day.

L et you use their stuff
I ntimate secrets shared.
F riends with you no matter what.
E very day they're always there to show you that they really care.

   My friends are Samantha and India.

Leila Edwards (11)
Ysgol Bryn Elian, Old Colwyn

Global

G lobal warming affects us all from
L osing our species to losing
O ur planet, by having
B ig floods
A nd thunderstorms too, and never able to
L ive to be older than we are now.

      If we keep going on
      In this habitat that we haven't known for very long.

Ross Thorpe (11)
Ysgol Bryn Elian, Old Colwyn

Music!

> Music, music everywhere.
> Chavs, emos, indie kids too.
> Festivals here, festivals there.
> Many bands don't know who to choose.

New wave, rap, indie, punk, pop.
Different ways you can dress.
Many programmes to watch,
Choose the right one to make the rest impressed.

> Pressure from all ways,
> Bullied if you're wrong.
> Girls covering their faces,
> Or just hiding in disgrace.

Most idols cause disruption,
Videos worst for distraction.
Minds brainwashed with wrong things,
You and others the effect it brings.

Calum Ryan (12)
Ysgol Bryn Elian, Old Colwyn

My Generation

> > *B* ullying is wrong in many ways
> And it affects *U* s all.

Bullying ruins the *L* ives of everyone.
> And bott *L* ing it up doesn't help either.
> > *Y* ou need to tell someone you trust
> > *I* f it's happening to you,
> They ca *N* help you
> > *G* et through it.

Kayleigh Harris (12)
Ysgol Bryn Elian, Old Colwyn

Crime

In the news,
In the newspaper,
It's everywhere.
Crime!

People are being murdered,
Some commit suicide,
It's everywhere.
Crime!

People don't feel safe,
Hoodies are being watched,
Waiting, lurking in the darkness.
Crime!

Everyone is blaming the police,
Now's the time to act,
It's everywhere.
Crime!

It will get us nowhere,
But people don't think,
It's everywhere.
Crime.

In the darkness, guns are fired,
In the twilight, wars rage on,
It's everywhere.
Crime!

Crime is blind as a bat,
Open your eyes, why do you do it?
Do you do it for fun?
Crime!

Knives suck the life out of people,
As they plunge into the victim,
The bullets squeal as the bang is heard,
How much longer can we go on?
Now's the time to act!
Crime!

It will get us nowhere!

Thomas Walsh (13)
Ysgol Bryn Elian, Old Colwyn

Celebrities

Botox, Botox,
they think it's wonderful.

Botox, Botox, they think it's fab.
But when you stop having it
your face starts to sag!

Names become fables
because they design
their own labels.

Size 0s, they think they're heroes
but they're not.

Drama queens,
stare in mirrors
and they wonder
why everything glitters!

Eleri Evans (11)
Ysgol Bryn Elian, Old Colwyn

Torture

Animals are great
They make good mates
But cruelty is around
Surely it will be found.

Horses you can ride
They always stay by your side
But kill them people do
You're lucky it's not you.

Cats are the *purr-fect* pets
But people tie them up in nets
Some get stoned
Others are just skin and bones.

Rats and mice are kept in cages
Just so people get their wages
Injections put in their sides and backs
And sadly they get put in sacks.

Dogs are said to be Man's best friend
But why do people drive them round the bend?
Showing teeth and growling voice
But sadly they don't have a choice.

Lions and tigers get shot down dead
While other animals lie in their beds
Pulled-off skins and heads on walls
While all the poachers have a ball.

Baby animals cut and skinned
While all their organs get thrown in bins
Sent to the butcher's, can't be late
Just so it can go on our plates!

It's torture!

Kora Hardern-Riley (13)
Ysgol Bryn Elian, Old Colwyn

Labels

Why do people judge us?
Everyone has to be in a group
Everyone gets labelled
We should all be individual

When people think of nerds they think:
Star Trek lover
Book reader
Smart person

When people think of chavs they think:
Tracksuit bottoms
Gold chains
Gangster rap

When people think of goths they think:
Black clothes
Piercings
Pale skin

When people think of emos they think:
Wrist slitting
Crying in a corner
Depression

When people think of skaters they think:
Skateboard in hand
Baggy clothes
Long hair

People should do what they want
After all, it's their choice.

Jack Williams (13)
Ysgol Bryn Elian, Old Colwyn

Police

Police, police are so great,
They arrest people to make them great!

Robbers, robbers steal cars,
But afterwards they are behind bars!

People, people think police are poo,
But they don't know who they are talking to!

Kids, kids think police are a pain,
They stop them playing their games!

Police, police their sirens blare,
They drive so fast and they even care!

Robbers, robbers they don't care,
Bumping cars they get so scared!

People, people watch how they drive,
As cameras watch to save their lives!

Kids, kids have no respect,
Until the police give them an ASBO!

Steven Jones (13)
Ysgol Bryn Elian, Old Colwyn

Playing

P laying out with my friends.
L aughing with them
A nd riding on a bike.
Y elling and screaming.
I t feels like I'm on a motorbike.
N ew bike in the light.
G et told off by the neighbours.

Dominik Fidor (13)
Ysgol Bryn Elian, Old Colwyn

Trapped

Go past the stars and through the sky.
Go under trees and through the leaves.
Go higher than hills and through the clouds.
Go open the door and along the floor.
Dodge the lightning, beat the wind.
Into the temple, through the walls,
And through another, along the halls.
So here I am, all alone.
That's where, inside a dome.
I am trapped and far from home.
That's where I am, hidden deep,
Underneath the big blue sea.
That's where you'll find me, hidden below,
Underneath the ice and snow.
So here I am, all alone.
Into darkness, away from light.
That's where I'm hiding, day and night!

James Davies (12)
Ysgol Bryn Elian, Old Colwyn

Environment

E veryone should look after the Earth.
N obody should litter.
V ery healthy Earth, we make it unhealthy.
I gnorant people pollute the Earth.
R ecycle rubbish, tins, cans, paper and clothes.
O ne cannot save the Earth.
N ext the Earth will explode.
M any people will die.
E veryone can help save the Earth.
N obody can make it worse, if we help
T hen the world will be saved!

Amy Miller (11)
Ysgol Bryn Elian, Old Colwyn

Global Warming, Stop It!

Global warming
There is no warning
That it comes this morning
Because of global warming

The seas, Earth and warmth
It's gonna kill us all
Even my friend Paul
Who isn't very tall

The wind makes tornadoes
Although they're unmanageable
People survive
But old people die!

Tsunamis are cool
But don't be fooled
They can kill
Just like a certain pill

Earthquakes strike
So be alright
As tonight
You might get a fright

The ice is melting
And polar bears are dying
Please do save them!
Because they won't last!

Daniel Thomas (13)
Ysgol Bryn Elian, Old Colwyn

My Sisters

One big
two small
oh help!
I can't handle them all!

Katie's a stroppy teenager,
so Mum says!
Shouting, screaming in
her new strange ways.

Tesni is a tiger
cute and sweet
at first sight
but will bite your head off
at the first fright.

Zoe's a little devil in disguise,
charms everyone to the full
right under their eyes.
But when she's alone
she changes her tone.

Even though they can be
annoying and mean
I love them all to bits
and they make my
heart gleam.

Sadie Boughen (11)
Ysgol Bryn Elian, Old Colwyn

Young Smokers

Smoking, smoking
Bad for your heart
The more you smoke
The more you look older.

Yellow teeth, yellow nails
You might think you look cool
But really inside you are harming yourself
And it is hard to give up
But you know you can.

Smoking and choking
Stinking and not thinking
It's a bad habit
Get out of it now!

Get yourself sorted
Stuff the cigs
Get some mates
Have the time of your life
It's what you deserve.

You think you look cool
With a fag in your hand
But now with new laws
You stand with closed doors.

Well I hope this poem
Will make you think
It isn't cool
It really stinks!

Bethany Ellis (13)
Ysgol Bryn Elian, Old Colwyn

War

When men are torn away from families
to defend their beloved country
not knowing if they will return
to feel the warmth of their family

People die every day
defending what is theirs
how long must this go on?
What will become of war?

Different countries fall out
over small or large issues.
Why can't we live in peace?
We all ask ourselves that!

Children ask where are their dads
whilst mothers grieve over graves
'Is all of this worth fighting for?'
Is the hardest question of all!

All that every soldier wants
and what every soldier deserves
is to die a hero.
And to know that their country loves them
as much as we love it!

Toby Whitehead (14)
Ysgol Bryn Elian, Old Colwyn

Abuse

My name is Lee,
My mummy never wanted me,
Daddy gave her drugs,
Now I'm here in a home full of thugs.

This children's home in Jersey,
Is the Devil's work,
The people who run it
Are jerks.

They let the staff beat me,
It hurts like hell,
They've tied me to a wall,
In the basement cell.

I'm still in the cell,
I see nothing, I've lost my sight,
I'm still hurting,
And I'll never be alright.

Through the darkness is a bright light,
It's beckoning me closer,
I know it's death,
If I go, I'll be alright . . .

They came for my body in the cell,
In the dead of night, nobody could tell,
What went on here, in this home,
No one will find my bones.

Danielle Louise Beddow (12)
Ysgol Bryn Elian, Old Colwyn

War

Publicity here, publicity there,
What's the point in it?
Hardly anyone cares.
People protecting us, helping us through,
All for us to turn our telly off at noon.
Families worrying, crying for you,
Waiting for their sons,
Their fate could happen soon.
Bombs flying here, bombs flying there,
Hopefully and maybe,
The soldiers will live another day,
But, does the government *really* even care?

Kayleigh Lewis (13)
Ysgol Bryn Elian, Old Colwyn

My Horse And Me

Pressing my knees to her sides,
She understands as we glide,
First a walk, then a gallop so fast,
To race the shadow that we cast.

We run and run,
Because it's fun.
Like rolling waves across the sea,
In perfect rhythm, my horse and me,
Always together,
Friends forever.

Keeley Trow (12)
Ysgol Bryn Elian, Old Colwyn

My Big Bro

They think they're it,
but they're not a bit.
They hit and kick
in a tick.

Living on the Xbox,
and throwing smelly socks.
Never willing to help,
driving me up the Alps.

Always playing football,
and never in the mall.
Goody-goody-two-shoes,
always on the loose.

I should like my big brother,
after all he's like no other,
even tho' he can be a pain
but knows when he's got something to gain.

Sarah Wynne-Williams (12)
Ysgol Bryn Elian, Old Colwyn

The Great Game

There's no time for homework, it's out for the game
It's a race to the end to see who gets fame
I go back in for tea
Then on to Liverpool FC

There's no time to waste with TV and stuff
It's out on the field where it all gets rough . . .
I was getting annoyed so I went in hard
The ref called me over and gave me a card

I shot the ball, the keeper saved
From that moment on I misbehaved
I love the game, the game that is great
Except for the losing, the losing I
                                          Hate!

David Parry (12)
Ysgol Bryn Elian, Old Colwyn

Pollution

Pollution, well what can I say?
It is wrecking our planet every day.

People dropping litter,
Makes me feel so bitter.

Big cars pumping out their fumes.
Don't they know disaster looms?

Ice caps melting day by day
Polar bears will be the ones who pay.

If we all just open our eyes and see
What a beautiful place our world could be.

Recycling and working together is the key
Then our world will live in peace and harmony.

Lucy Jones (12)
Ysgol Bryn Elian, Old Colwyn

The World

Death, war, racism and hate,
Why can't everyone just be mates?
Divorce, marriage break-ups and affairs,
Nobody really seems to care.

Fame, fortune, money and news,
Is all people care about as well as booze.
Drugs, hate and needless violence,
Is there hope for any silence?

Blood, crime, thrill and gore,
Does the world have hope anymore?
I don't think so, why can't we help?
Because all people want is fame and wealth.

Joseph Rickard (12)
Ysgol Bryn Elian, Old Colwyn

The World Today

We look around,
What do we see?
Polluted ground
And litter in the sea.

                We watch the news,
                What do we hear?
                The people we lose.
                The people we fear.

We hear the stories,
We hear them clear.
The battle of the Tories,
And the lies we hear.

                We see the children,
                We watch them grow.
                They like having fun
                But they will never know . . .

The pain we go through,
What we've lived in,
The horror we know too.
The world full of sin.

                But what can we do?
                We can only sit and wait
                Until the day someone decides to act.
                The world needs to change *now*
                And that's a fact!

Corrin Treleaven-Westwood (12)
Ysgol Bryn Elian, Old Colwyn

A Broken Message

From Courtney

A broken message
A broken heart
Find the key
To unlock your heart.

Find the form
With the key
Find the empathy
Then you'll see
You and me
Were meant to be.

You have your mates
I have mine
If we break
We'll both be fine.

I am the broken message
I have the broken heart
I can't find the key
To unlock your heart

End message.

Courtney Giblin (13)
Ysgol Bryn Elian, Old Colwyn

Celebrities

Some celebrities are not who you think they are,
They drive around drunk crashing their flashy cars,
Most of them ending up behind bars.

A lot of celebrities take drugs, drink booze, take up smoking,
All these things will leave you choking,
Honestly, I am not joking!

They go around showing off their money,
But it all ends up down the dunny,
It really isn't funny!

Celebrities have dolled-up faces,
Found in hundreds of different places,
Causing police and celebrity chases.

You may think celebrities are fantastic,
But they all look like plastic.
Don't copy them!

Caitlin Baxter (11)
Ysgol Bryn Elian, Old Colwyn

War

Children crying for their family.
Everyone's gone to war.
Guns shooting loud and clear.
People getting wounded, more and more.
Hospitals full of people injured.
Some die, what can they do?
There is not enough medication to go round.
What should we do?

Jade Louise Griffiths (12)
Ysgol Bryn Elian, Old Colwyn

Cars

Cars, cars, everywhere.
Everybody looks with an eager stare.
You see them at night with their neon lights.
You see them in the street with a low light.

The sports cars go faster than a rocket.
The slow cars go slower than a thief emptying a pocket.
The 4x4s bump off road.
The normal cars follow the herd.

When the cars crash,
There's a *big* smash.
All the metal is crunched and jarred.
Then they take it to the scrap yard.

Cars are like rockets.
Cars crash and smash.
Cars are fast like rockets.
Lives and cars are turned to trash.

Denzel Simon (14)
Ysgol Bryn Elian, Old Colwyn

People

People don't get bullied
People recycle for the environment
People get a loving family
People have friends to talk to
People have jobs to attend
People have school to attend
People make money
People are loved from birth to death.
People . . . one of us!

Alec Jones (12)
Ysgol Bryn Elian, Old Colwyn

Little Boys (My Brother)

Little boys, what can I say?
They do absolutely nothing but play all day,
Leaving the work to us girls,
We clean everything till they look like pearls.

Snotty noses and mud up their legs,
Then they just say, 'I'm tired and I'm going to bed.'
We go into their room and, oh my gosh,
We nearly collapse, it's like a smelly old bog!

Trainers, toys and clothes everywhere,
Guess who has to tidy them away? It just isn't fair!
PlayStation, telly, all the time,
I mean those things are even part mine!

Little boys, what can I say?
But I'd be nothing if mine wasn't there every day!

Chloe Mangnall (11)
Ysgol Bryn Elian, Old Colwyn

School

School is boring
School is boring
When I'm in school I feel like snoring
What's the point of uniform
When we can wear our own clothes?

Maths, English, science
We should form an alliance.

School is boring
School is boring
When I'm in school, I feel like snoring
What's the point of school,
It only makes me drool.

Connor Nichols (12)
Ysgol Bryn Elian, Old Colwyn

The Planet

The planet is our only one
But soon, guess what? It shall be gone.
Pollution is here
So the sea is no longer clear.

Pandas, polar bears, penguins too
They all need the help that comes from you.
In the future we will all feel blue
For the only place you'll see them is the zoo.

Bottles and glass, paper and tins
Recycling needs to happen,
And it starts with us
For the future generation to be happy.

Cars and lorries come off the road.
Exhaust pipes, wheels, the Highway Code.
Fumes of petrol like smoke from a fire
Climbing higher, higher and higher.

Things that will happen, well, it's endless
The planet is dying right before our eyes unless,
We save it right *now!*

Bethany Starr (11)
Ysgol Bryn Elian, Old Colwyn

Climbing

C limbing up trees
L eaping over rivers
I n the bushes I hide
M essing with sticks in the trees
B ut getting stuck up the tree
I t starts to get dark
N ear the swamp I stand
G etting stuck in the mud and crying.

Darren Arthur (12)
Ysgol Bryn Elian, Old Colwyn

Why Oh Why Did He Go To War?

A young boy goes to war,
He doesn't know what he's in for,
Death and violence are through the door,
Why oh why did he go to war?

His family says what a shame,
But who, oh who, must we blame
As the bullets leave the chain?
Why oh why did he go to war?

What if he dies?
Tears and cries?
Is he just like all the other guys?
Why oh why did he go to war?

Is he a hero
Or is he a zero?
Will they give him a cheer, oh,
When will he come back through that door?

Will they knock on the door,
Or call on the phone?
Will he come back a king on a throne?
Why oh why did he go to war? . . .

It was about one o'clock
When I got the knock
I started to cry
I asked why did he die?
I ran out of the door,
Why oh why did he go to war?

Tristan Rowllings (13)
Ysgol Bryn Elian, Old Colwyn

The Dream Team

Fabregas, what a player,
His rhythm is mind-blowing,
His skills are as good as Picasso's paintings,
What can you say? He's brilliant!

Almunia to Gallas,
Gallas to Fabregas,
Fabregas to Adebayor,
It's a goal!

Walcott, what an athlete,
He can make players look like idiots,
He's as fast as a cheetah,
Is that enough of an explanation?

Alumnia to Gallas
Gallas to Flamini
Flamini to Walcott
Obviously, it's a goal!

Gallas, what a defender,
If you try to get past him,
He's like a tonne of bricks coming down on you,
He's as tough as a stone,
What more can you say, he's brilliant!

Alumnia to Gallas
Gallas to Hleb
Hleb to Eduardo
What a goal!

Edward John Roberts (13)
Ysgol Bryn Elian, Old Colwyn

School!

School, school, it's just not fair,
No mobiles, uniform, no fun!
The bullies, the detentions, the writing,
The 'everything wrong' and the 'nothing right'!

What's all this uniform business?
Where's the point in it?
We should wear our choice of clothes,
Not the 'oh so special' teachers' choice!

Where are all the servants, the plasma screens?
Where are all the amusements and entertainment?
Instead, we sit down in classrooms working!
We listen and read, then we listen and write!

Why aren't we even allowed mobiles?
What's going on?
What are we meant to do for a laugh?
What are we meant to do with our mates?

Where are all the pools, the cinemas and rides?
The game rooms, the stadiums and the tracks
Where's any of that?
Where's any of the fun?

School, school, it's just not fair,
No mobiles, uniform, no fun!
The bullies, the detentions, the writing,
The 'everything wrong' and the 'nothing right'!

Robert Richards (13)
Ysgol Bryn Elian, Old Colwyn

Oh Why, Oh Why?

Oh why, oh why are we lazy?
Oh why, oh why are we lazy?
In a few years our world will die,
And we will all have nowhere to lie

Men on the streets will cry
And why are we just too shy
To give them money, it's just not funny
Oh why oh why are we killing our world?
Oh why, oh why are we killing our world?
All around us we are killing and killing,
And we will go on till there's nothing left to kill
We will fill the world with our rubbish
We are too free to be rubbish

Oh why, oh why, do polar bears die?
Oh why, oh why, do polar bears die?
It's not fair, don't sit back or lie down
Take it to action and stand that ground
We take our cars to go round and round.
Don't be selfish and take some action.
Turn off your lights and turn off your TV.
Oh why, oh why, do we have to die?
Oh why, oh why, do we have to die?
Do something now
Don't let our children die!

Kyle Heath (12)
Ysgol Bryn Elian, Old Colwyn

Cars

Fast cars everywhere.
Fast cars everywhere.

Zooming past without much care.
As fast as a rocket, people stop and stare.

At night they prowl like a cat.
In the day they are as loud as a bat.

White cars, black cars, green cars, blue.
Rushing around and speeding past you.

The fast cars cause almighty crashes.
The slow cars cause little smashes.

Fast cars everywhere.
Fast cars everywhere.

Young people drive fast for a dare.
Old people drive slow for a stare!

Tomos Williams (13)
Ysgol Bryn Elian, Old Colwyn

Size Zero!

You're seen as a fake fashion hero
But only if you've achieved the size zero
But why people want to be that way
I really don't know, they just won't say.

They're obsessed with make-up,
Guys and fashion.
But they're really just dolls with a passion.

They just don't get why people feel under the threat.
With their pathetic plastic, powdered faces
When they leave their sarcastic traces.

Little do they know as they start to grow
You become who you really are
And will be happier by far with whom you are.

Holly Griffith (13)
Ysgol Bryn Elian, Old Colwyn

Violence

Brawling, fighting, pain and crying,
Violence is pointless you can end up dying,
There's theft on the streets,
And threats in the shops,
LFC fight in the Liverpool Cop.
The police try hard every day
To make all those bad criminals pay.
There is a growing rate of drug abuse,
People should think about the path they choose.
Alcohol, fags, weed, glue and speed,
Damage people and those around them.
Brawling, fighting, pain and crying,
Violence is pointless you can end up dying!

Stephen Toseland (12)
Ysgol Bryn Elian, Old Colwyn

Bullies

B ullies are hurtful
  They want to make us cry alone.

U gly nasty things.
  We just want to fly away and leave the horror behind.

L iving in shame as your heart crashes to the floor.

L onely, with no one to turn to in your hour of need.

I n hand, in hand, you block your trouble away.

E nd is near while you want to commit suicide.

S top them while you are ahead.
  Shout aloud, *not* in your head.

Kelly Anne Marsden (11)
Ysgol Bryn Elian, Old Colwyn

My World

My world was once beautiful,
but not anymore
as factories pollute it
and so much more . . .

Poverty is quite normal now
as there are millions to feed
hungry bellies are weeping
in desperate need.

Ice caps are melting as we speak.
The polar bears are getting weak.
The children are crying.
God's creatures are dying.

So let's give a helping hand
and start recycling!

Samantha Farah (12)
Ysgol Bryn Elian, Old Colwyn

Poverty

Youngsters searching
Hungry and ill
Homeless and weary
Fighting for a slab to sleep on

Horrible guns
War and conflict
Loud noises and scary places
This is poverty, *child poverty!*

Natalie Hughes (12)
Ysgol Bryn Elian, Old Colwyn

The Red Star

All day I wait,
to escape
from this school,
that's not so cool.

I wait till night,
as the light,
it fades to dark
and leaves a mark.

I look up at the star
that is so far
I'd like to see
that burning sea

I see the figure
the stars that flicker
Gliese is the name
that'll stay the same.

Phillip Roberts (12)
Ysgol Bryn Elian, Old Colwyn

Bullying

In school.
In the local park.
In alleys.
In the world.
Horrible things happen
Not just to you.
To everyone they bully
To get attention, to get power.
They have no friends, you do.
So don't do something silly.

Ashley Holden (11)
Ysgol Bryn Elian, Old Colwyn

Fake

Pretty girls
Synthetic curls

Porcelain faces
Lipstick traces

Pearly whites
Vicious cat fights

Being 'cool'
Dodging school

Treat 'em mean
Keep 'em keen.

Their diamonds are plastic.
Their attitudes unenthusiastic -

They're fake!

Callum Hughes (13)
Ysgol Bryn Elian, Old Colwyn

Wars, Horrific Wars

Wars, horrific wars!
Death around every door.

Young and old go off to fight,
For what they think is right.

Maybe they should think a bit,
Before they pick up their army kit.

WWI, WWII, Hitler murdering every Jew,
He thought he was right too!

Why can't we just live in peace?
Stop the fighting and pain at least.

Chris Fowler (14)
Ysgol Bryn Elian, Old Colwyn

Here And Now

Uniforms, uniforms
Why do we wear them?
They cost so much
Why don't we just burn them?

Uniforms, uniforms,
They are so plain,
We are just involved
In this huge, silly game!

Uniforms, uniforms,
We are all classed as one,
I really don't like it,
It's a very big con!

Uniforms, uniforms,
Why do we wear them?
They cost so much,
Why don't we just burn them?

Steph Dennis (14)
Ysgol Bryn Elian, Old Colwyn

Grandma

My grandma likes to knit,
On her rocking chair she sits.
Needles in her hand,
She always feels so grand.
I love my grandma lots and lots,
I'll even help her with the pots.
Every day I'll always say,
'You're the greatest in every way!'

Ellesse Lauren Lynch (12)
Ysgol Bryn Elian, Old Colwyn

Bullying Is Wrong

Bullying, bullying
Bullying is wrong
The more you bully
The more people become harmed.

> Bullying, bullying
> Bullies are wrong
> They should be locked up
> And the keys should be thrown.

Bullying, bullying
Bullying needs to stop
The more people get bullied
The more they commit suicide.

> Bullying, bullying
> Bullying is bad
> It's mostly the boys
> That make you feel so sad.

Bullying, bullying
Bullying isn't nice
Girls have problems
Boys are like mice.

> Bullying, bullying
> Is just a waste of time
> Get up and sort yourselves out
> There's no need for bullies.

Bullying, bullying
Bullying is pathetic
There's no need for it
You just lose your friends.

> You might think it's to get new friends
> Or just to fit in but really it makes you offend.

Heidi Leanne Ellis (13)
Ysgol Bryn Elian, Old Colwyn

Style

Style is everything today,
and it has changed in every way.
Style, from puffy trousers,
and things that make you go *wowsers!*

People try to have style,
but they're off by a mile!
Sometimes they look cool,
but sometimes they look a fool.

A lot of colours have been used,
even the hippies got confused!
In the end they got it right,
but today, it's better to wear white.

From Debenhams to Peacocks,
We rely on them to give us our socks.
We want it all at low prices,
But we're in the middle of a credit crisis.

Style, style, everywhere,
why does anyone care?

Nicholas Ledden (12)
Ysgol Bryn Elian, Old Colwyn

Cancer

So many types,
Why do so many people die?
I think our government spends too much money on wars
Instead of on hospitals and funding for cures.
If we had check-ups to catch it while it's small,
My Taid would still be here, to talk once more.

Glen Urquhart (12)
Ysgol Bryn Elian, Old Colwyn

Young Writers Information

We hope you have enjoyed reading this book - and that you will continue to enjoy it in the coming years.

If you like reading and writing poetry drop us a line, or give us a call, and we'll send you a free information pack.

Alternatively if you would like to order further copies of this book or any of our other titles, then please give us a call or log onto our website at www.youngwriters.co.uk

Young Writers Information
Remus House
Coltsfoot Drive
Peterborough
PE2 9JX

(01733) 890066